the BIG book of baby AFGHANS

LEISURE ARTS, INC.
Maumelle, Arkansas

EDITORIAL STAFF
Editor-in-Chief: Susan White Sullivan
Director of Designer Relations: Cheryl Johnson
Special Projects Director: Susan Frantz Wiles
Senior Prepress Director: Mark Hawkins
Art Publications Director: Rhonda Shelby
Technical Editor: Linda A. Daley
Technical Writers: Sarah J. Green and
    Lois J. Long
Editorial Writer: Susan McManus Johnson
Senior Graphic Artist: Lora Puls
Graphic Artist: Becca Snider
Imaging Technician: Stephanie Johnson
Prepress Technician: Janie Marie Wright
Photography Manager: Katherine Laughlin
Contributing Photographer: Ken West
Contributing Photostylist: Sondra Daniel
Publishing Systems Administrator: Becky Riddle
Mac Information Technology Specialist:
    Robert Young

BUSINESS STAFF
President and Chief Executive Officer:
    Rick Barton
Vice President and Chief Operations Officer:
    Tom Siebenmorgen
Vice President of Sales: Mike Behar
Director of Finance and Administration:
    Laticia Mull Dittrich
National Sales Director: Martha Adams
Creative Services: Chaska Lucas
Information Technology Director: Hermine Linz
Controller: Francis Caple
Vice President, Operations: Jim Dittrich
Retail Customer Service Manager: Stan Raynor
Print Production Manager: Fred F. Pruss

Library of Congress Control Number:
    2011925031
ISBN-13: 978-1-60900-143-8

table of CONTENTS

You'll find 29 adorable designs to crochet in this big collection of baby blankets! These patterns are classics from the Leisure Arts library, each one created by a popular designer. Choose the quiet elegance of lace or pick a burst of bright motifs. There are wavy panels and lovely pattern stitch afghans. All are perfect for baby shower gifts! Some of the larger designs would also make thoughtful first-birthday presents. Let the clear instructions and sweet photos inspire you to make a very special baby blanket for that wonderful little person in your life.

baby blue

■■□□ EASY

Finished Size: 33" x 44½" (84 cm x 113 cm)

MATERIALS
Medium Weight Yarn **(4)** MEDIUM
[3 ounces, 192 yards
(85 grams, 175 meters) per skein]:
  6 skeins
Crochet hook, size J (6 mm) **or** size needed
  for gauge

GAUGE: In pattern, 2 repeats = 4¼" (10.75 cm)
and 8 rows = 4" (10 cm)

Gauge Swatch: 6"w x 4¾"h (15.25 cm x 12 cm)
Ch 24.
Work same as Afghan Body Rows 1-9.
Finish off.

STITCH GUIDE

DECREASE (uses 2 sps)
First Leg: YO, insert hook in same sp as last st
made, YO and pull up a loop, YO and draw through
2 loops on hook (2 loops remaining on hook).
Second Leg: YO, insert hook in next ch-3 sp, YO
and pull up a loop, YO and draw through 2 loops on
hook, YO and draw through all 3 loops on hook.
PICOT
Ch 3, slip st in third ch from hook.

AFGHAN BODY
Ch 96.

Row 1 (Right side): Sc in second ch from hook, skip
next 2 chs, dc in next ch, (ch 1, dc in same ch) twice,
skip next 2 chs, sc in next ch, ★ ch 3, skip next ch, sc in
next ch, skip next 2 chs, dc in next ch, (ch 1, dc in same
ch) twice, skip next 2 chs, sc in next ch; repeat from ★
across: 60 sts and 35 sps.

Row 2: Ch 5 (**counts as first dc plus ch 2**), turn; sc
in next ch-1 sp, ch 3, sc in next ch-1 sp, ★ dc in next
ch-3 sp, (ch 1, dc in same sp) twice, sc in next ch-1 sp,
ch 3, sc in next ch-1 sp; repeat from ★ across, ch 2, skip
next dc, dc in last sc: 59 sts and 36 sps.

Row 3: Ch 1, turn; sc in first dc, skip next ch-2 sp, dc in
next ch-3 sp, (ch 1, dc in same sp) twice, ★ sc in next
ch-1 sp, ch 3, sc in next ch-1 sp, dc in next ch-3 sp,
(ch 1, dc in same sp) twice; repeat from ★ across to last
ch-2 sp, skip last ch-2 sp, sc in last dc: 60 sts and 35 sps.

Repeat Rows 2 and 3 for pattern until Afghan Body
measures approximately 36½" (92.5 cm) from beginning
ch, ending by working Row 3; at end of last row, do **not**
finish off.

EDGING

Rnd 1: Ch 1, do **not** turn; 2 sc in last sc made; working
around st at end of rows, work 115 sc evenly spaced
across; 3 sc in free loop of first ch of beginning ch
(*Fig. 2b, page 91*), 4 sc in next sp, 3 sc in next sp, sc in
next sp, (3 sc in each of next 2 sps, sc in next sp) across
to last 2 sps, 3 sc in next sp, 4 sc in last sp, 3 sc in free
loop of ch at base of last sc; working around st at end of
rows, work 115 sc evenly spaced across; working across
last row, 3 sc in first sc, [sc in next dc, (sc in next ch-1 sp
and in next next dc) twice, 2 sc in next ch-3 sp, skip next
sc] twice, sc in next dc, (sc in next ch-1 sp and in next
dc) twice, ★ 3 sc in next ch-3 sp, [skip next sc, sc in next
dc, (sc in next ch-1 sp and in next dc) twice, 2 sc in next
ch-3 sp] twice, skip next sc, sc in next dc, (sc in next
ch-1 sp and in next dc) twice; repeat from ★ 2 times
more, sc in same st as first sc; join with slip st to first sc:
412 sc.

Rnd 2: Ch 1, (sc, ch 3) twice in same st, ★ skip next
sc, (sc in next sc, ch 3, skip next sc) across to center sc
of next corner 3-sc group, (sc, ch 3) twice in center sc;
repeat from ★ 2 times **more**, skip next sc, (sc in next
sc, ch 3, skip next sc) across; join with slip st to first sc:
210 ch-3 sps.

Rnds 3-5: Slip st in next corner ch-3 sp, ch 1, (sc, ch 3) twice in same sp, ★ (sc in next ch-3 sp, ch 3) across to next corner ch-3 sp, (sc, ch 3) twice in corner ch-3 sp; repeat from ★ 2 times **more**, (sc in next ch-3 sp, ch 3) across; join with slip st to first sc: 222 ch-3 sps.

Rnd 6: Slip st in next corner ch-3 sp, ch 6, (decrease, ch 3) around, hdc in same sp as Second Leg of last decrease made; join with slip st to third ch of beginning ch-6.

Rnds 7-9: Slip st in next corner ch-3 sp, ch 1, (sc, ch 3) twice in same sp, ★ (sc in next ch-3 sp, ch 3) across to next corner ch-3 sp, (sc, ch 3) twice in corner ch-3 sp; repeat from ★ 2 times **more**, (sc in next ch-3 sp, ch 3) across; join with slip st to first sc: 234 ch-3 sps.

Rnd 10: (Slip st, ch 4, dc) in next corner ch-3 sp, (ch 1, dc in same sp) 3 times, ★ † sc in next ch-3 sp, ch 3, sc in next ch-3 sp, [dc in next ch-3 sp, (ch 1, dc in same sp) twice, sc in next ch-3 sp, ch 3, sc in next ch-3 sp] across to next corner ch-3 sp †, dc in corner ch-3 sp, (ch 1, dc in same sp) 4 times; repeat from ★ 2 times **more**, then repeat from † to † once; join with slip st to first dc: 78 ch-3 sps.

Rnd 11: Ch 6, slip st in third ch from hook, ★ † (dc in next ch-1 sp, work Picot) 4 times, dc in next dc, sc in next ch-3 sp, skip next sc, [dc in next dc, work Picot, (dc in next ch-1 sp, work Picot) twice, dc in next dc, sc in next ch-3 sp, skip next sc] across to next corner 5-dc group †, dc in next dc, work Picot; repeat from ★ 2 times **more**, then repeat from † to † once; join with slip st to third ch of beginning ch-6, finish off.

Design by Kay Meadors. ●

cluster **stripes**

◼◼◻◻ EASY

Finished Size: 38" x 50" (96.5 cm x 127 cm)

MATERIALS

Medium Weight Yarn 🏷**4**

[3.5 ounces, 241 yards
(100 grams, 220 meters) per skein]:
    White - 2 skeins
    Lavender - 2 skeins
    Blue - 2 skeins
    Green - 2 skeins
Crochet hook, size I (5.5 mm) **or** size needed
    for gauge

GAUGE: In pattern, 2 repeats = 4" (10 cm)
            and 8 rows = 6" (15.25 cm)

Gauge Swatch: 5½"w x 6"h (14 cm x 15.25 cm)
With White, ch 27.
Work same as Afghan Body Rows 1-8.

STITCH GUIDE

CLUSTER (uses next 5 sts)
YO, insert hook in next dc, YO and pull up a loop,
YO and draw through 2 loops on hook, ★ YO, insert
hook in **next** ch, YO and pull up a loop, YO and draw
through 2 loops on hook, YO, insert hook in **next** st,
YO and pull up a loop, YO and draw through 2 loops
on hook; repeat from ★ once **more**, YO and draw
through all 6 loops on hook.
DECREASE (uses last 2 dc)
★ YO, insert hook in **next** dc, YO and pull up a loop,
YO and draw through 2 loops on hook; repeat from
★ once **more**, YO and draw through all 3 loops on
hook **(counts as one dc)**.
PICOT
Ch 3, hdc in third ch from hook.
SCALLOP
Ch 3, dc in third ch from hook.

AFGHAN BODY

With White, ch 155; place marker in third ch from hook
for st placement.

Row 1: Dc in fifth ch from hook, ch 1, skip next ch, (dc,
ch 3, dc) in next ch, ch 1, ★ skip next ch, work Cluster,
ch 1, skip next ch, (dc, ch 3, dc) in next ch, ch 1; repeat
from ★ across to last 4 chs, (YO, skip **next** ch, insert
hook in **next** ch, YO and pull up a loop, YO and draw
through 2 loops on hook) twice, YO and draw through all
3 loops on hook: 18 Clusters.

Row 2 (Right side)**:** Ch 2, turn; dc in next dc, ch 1, (dc,
ch 3, dc) in next ch-3 sp, ch 1, ★ work Cluster, ch 1, (dc,
ch 3, dc) in next ch-3 sp, ch 1; repeat from ★ across to
last 2 dc, decrease; finish off.

Note: Loop a short piece of yarn around any stitch to
mark Row 2 as **right** side.

Row 3: With **wrong** side facing, join Lavender with
slip st in first dc; ch 2, dc in next dc, ch 1, (dc, ch 3, dc)
in next ch-3 sp, ch 1, ★ work Cluster, ch 1, (dc, ch 3, dc)
in next ch-3 sp, ch 1; repeat from ★ across to last 2 dc,
decrease; do **not** finish off.

Row 4: Ch 2, turn; dc in next dc, ch 1, (dc, ch 3, dc) in
next ch-3 sp, ch 1, ★ work Cluster, ch 1, (dc, ch 3, dc)
in next ch-3 sp, ch 1; repeat from ★ across to last 2 dc,
decrease; finish off.

Rows 5 and 6: With Blue, repeat Rows 3 and 4.

Rows 7 and 8: With Green, repeat Rows 3 and 4.

Rows 9 and 10: With White, repeat Rows 3 and 4.

Rows 11-66: Repeat Rows 3-10, 7 times; at end of
Row 66, do **not** finish off.

EDGING

Ch 2, do **not** turn; working in end of rows, hdc in top of last dc made, (slip st, ch 2, hdc) in top of next row and in top of each row across; working in sps and in free loops of beginning ch **(Fig. 2b, page 91)**, (slip st, work Picot, slip st) in marked ch, work Scallop, skip next 2 chs, slip st in next sp, ch 1, slip st in next sp, work Scallop, ★ skip next 2 chs, (slip st, work Picot, slip st) in next ch, work Scallop, slip st in next sp, ch 1, slip st in next sp, work Scallop; repeat from ★ across to last 3 chs, skip next 2 chs, (slip st, work Picot, slip st, ch 2, hdc) in last ch; working in end of rows, (slip st, ch 2, hdc) in top of first row and in top of each row across to last row, skip last row; working across Row 66, slip st in first dc and in next ch-1 sp, work Scallop, (slip st, work Picot, slip st) in next ch-3 sp, work Scallop, slip st in next ch-1 sp, † ch 1, slip st in next ch-1 sp, work Scallop, (slip st, work Picot, slip st) in next ch-3 sp, work Scallop, slip st in next ch-1 sp †; repeat from † to † across to last dc; join with slip st in last dc, finish off.

Design by Anne Halliday. ●

baby loves springtime

■■■□ INTERMEDIATE

Finished Size: 37" (94 cm) square

MATERIALS

Light Weight Yarn **［3 LIGHT］**
[1.75 ounces, 161 yards
(50 grams, 147 meters) per skein**]**:
    Pink - 7 skeins
    Dk Pink - 3 skeins
    White - 3 skeins
Crochet hook, size F (3.75 mm) **or** size needed
    for gauge

GAUGE: In pattern,
    (3 dc, ch 1) 5 times = 4" (10 cm)
    and 7 sc rnds = 1½" (3.75 cm)

Gauge Swatch: 6" (15.25 cm) square
Work same as Afghan through Rnd 7.

AFGHAN

With Pink, ch 4; join with slip st to form a ring.

Rnd 1 (Right side)**:** Ch 3 **(counts as first dc, now and throughout)**, 2 dc in ring, (ch 2, 3 dc in ring) 3 times, hdc in first dc to form last ch-2 sp: 12 dc and 4 ch-2 sps.

Note: Loop a short piece of yarn around any stitch to mark Rnd 1 as **right** side.

Rnd 2: Ch 3, turn; 2 dc in last ch-2 sp made, ch 1, ★ (3 dc, ch 2, 3 dc) in next ch-2 sp, ch 1; repeat from ★ around, 3 dc in same sp as first dc, hdc in first dc to form last ch-2 sp: 8 3-dc groups and 8 sps.

Rnd 3: Ch 3, turn; 2 dc in last ch-2 sp made, ch 1, 3 dc in next ch-1 sp, ch 1, ★ (3 dc, ch 2, 3 dc) in next corner ch-2 sp, ch 1, 3 dc in next ch-1 sp, ch 1; repeat from ★ around, 3 dc in same sp as first dc, hdc in first dc to form last ch-2 sp: 12 3-dc groups and 12 sps.

Rnds 4-6: Ch 3, turn; 2 dc in last ch-2 sp made, ch 1, (3 dc in next ch-1 sp, ch 1) across to next corner ch-2 sp, ★ (3 dc, ch 2, 3 dc) in corner ch-2 sp, ch 1, (3 dc in next ch-1 sp, ch 1) across to next corner ch-2 sp; repeat from ★ around, 3 dc in same sp as first dc, hdc in first dc to form last ch-2 sp: 24 3-dc groups and 24 sps.

Rnd 7: Ch 3, turn; 2 dc in last ch-2 sp made, ch 1, (3 dc in next ch-1 sp, ch 1) across to next corner ch-2 sp, ★ (3 dc, ch 2, 3 dc) in corner ch-2 sp, ch 1, (3 dc in next ch-1 sp, ch 1) across to next corner ch-2 sp; repeat from ★ around, 3 dc in same sp as first dc, ch 2; join with slip st to first dc, finish off: 28 3-dc groups and 28 sps.

> When working with 2 colors on a round, work over unused color.

Rnd 8: With **right** side facing, working in Back Loops Only of dc and in chs **(Fig. 1, page 91)**, and working over White, join Dk Pink with sc in first ch of any corner ch-2 **(see Joining With Sc, page 91)**; ★ † ch 2, sc in next ch changing to White **(Fig. 5a, page 93)**, sc in next 9 sts changing to Dk Pink in last sc made, sc in next 9 sts changing to White in last sc made, sc in next 9 sts changing to Dk Pink in last sc made †, sc in next ch; repeat from ★ 2 times **more**, then repeat from † to † once; join with slip st to first sc: 116 sc and 4 ch-2 sps.

Rnd 9: Ch 1, do **not** turn; working in both loops, sc in same st as joining, ★ † (sc, ch 2, sc) in next corner ch-2 sp, sc in next sc changing to White, follow Chart 1 once (page 10) changing colors in same manner and changing to Dk Pink in last sc made †, sc in next sc; repeat from ★ 2 times **more**, then repeat from † to † once; join with slip st to first sc: 124 sc and 4 ch-2 sps.

Rnd 10: Ch 1, sc in same st as joining and in next sc, ★ † (2 sc, ch 2, 2 sc) in next corner ch-2 sp, sc in next 2 sc changing to White in last sc made, follow Chart 1 once changing to Dk Pink in last sc made †, sc in next 2 sc; repeat from ★ 2 times **more**, then repeat from † to † once; join with slip st to first sc: 140 sc and 4 ch-2 sps.

Instructions continued on page 10.

Rnds 11-14: Ch 1, sc in same st as joining and in each sc across to next corner ch-2 sp, ★ † (sc, ch 2, sc) in corner ch-2 sp, sc in each Dk Pink sc across changing to White in last sc made, follow Chart 1 once changing to Dk Pink in last sc made †, sc in each sc across to next corner ch-2 sp; repeat from ★ 2 times **more**, then repeat from † to † once; join with slip st to first sc: 172 sc and 4 ch-2 sps.

Finish off Dk Pink and cut White.

CHART 1

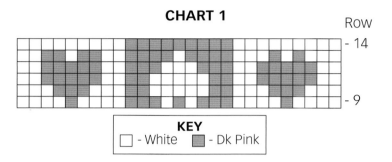

Row
- 14

- 9

| KEY |
| □ - White   ▨ - Dk Pink |

Rnd 15: With **wrong** side facing, join Pink with dc in any corner ch-2 sp *(see Joining With Dc, page 91)*; 2 dc in same sp, ch 1, skip next 3 sc, (3 dc in next sc, ch 1, skip next 3 sc) across to next corner ch-2 sp, ★ (3 dc, ch 2, 3 dc) in corner ch-2 sp, ch 1, skip next 3 sc, (3 dc in next sc, ch 1, skip next 3 sc) across to next corner ch-2 sp; repeat from ★ around, 3 dc in same sp as first dc, hdc in first dc to form last ch-2 sp: 48 3-dc groups and 48 sps.

Rnds 16-21: Ch 3, **turn**; 2 dc in last ch-2 sp made, ch 1, (3 dc in next ch-1 sp, ch 1) across to next corner ch-2 sp, ★ (3 dc, ch 2, 3 dc) in corner ch-2 sp, ch 1, (3 dc in next ch-1 sp, ch 1) across to next corner ch-2 sp; repeat from ★ around, 3 dc in same sp as first dc, hdc in first dc to form last ch-2 sp: 72 3-dc groups and 72 sps.

Rnd 22: Ch 3, turn; 2 dc in last ch-2 sp made, ch 1, (3 dc in next ch-1 sp, ch 1) across to next corner ch-2 sp, ★ (3 dc, ch 2, 3 dc) in corner ch-2 sp, ch 1, (3 dc in next ch-1 sp, ch 1) across to next corner ch-2 sp; repeat from ★ around, 3 dc in same sp as first dc, ch 2; join with slip st to first dc, finish off: 76 3-dc groups and 76 sps.

Rnd 23: With **right** side facing, working in Back Loops Only of dc and in chs, and working over Dk Pink, join White with sc in first ch of any corner ch-2; ★ † ch 2, sc in next ch changing to Dk Pink, sc in next 15 sts changing to White in last sc made, (sc in next 15 sts changing to Dk Pink in last sc made, sc in next 15 sts changing to White in last sc made) twice †, sc in next ch; repeat from ★ 2 times **more**, then repeat from † to † once; join with slip st to first sc: 308 sc and 4 ch-2 sps.

Rnd 24: Ch 1, do **not** turn; working in both loops, sc in same st as joining, ★ † (sc, ch 2, sc) in next corner ch-2 sp, sc in next sc changing to Dk Pink, follow Chart 2 (page 11) from A to C twice, then from A to B once changing to White in last sc made †, sc in next sc; repeat from ★ 2 times **more**, then repeat from † to † once; join with slip st to first sc: 316 sc and 4 ch-2 sps.

Rnd 25: Ch 1, sc in same st as joining and in next sc, ★ † (sc, ch 2, sc) in next corner ch-2 sp, sc in next 2 sc changing to Dk Pink in last sc made, follow Chart 2 from A to C twice, then from A to B once changing to White in last sc made †, sc in next 2 sc; repeat from ★ 2 times **more**, then repeat from † to † once; join with slip st to first sc: 324 sc and 4 ch-2 sps.

Rnd 26: Ch 1, sc in same st as joining and in next 2 sc, ★ † (2 sc, ch 2, 2 sc) in next corner ch-2 sp, sc in next 3 sc changing to Dk Pink in last sc made, follow Chart 2 from A to C twice, then from A to B once changing to White in last sc made †, sc in next 3 sc; repeat from ★ 2 times **more**, then repeat from † to † once; join with slip st to first sc: 340 sc and 4 ch-2 sps.

Rnds 27-35: Ch 1, sc in same st as joining and in each sc across to next corner ch-2 sp, ★ † (sc, ch 2, sc) in corner ch-2 sp, sc in each White sc across changing to Dk Pink in last sc made, follow Chart 2 from A to C twice, then from A to B once changing to White in last sc made †, sc in each sc across to next corner ch-2 sp; repeat from ★ 2 times **more**, then repeat from † to † once; join with slip st to first sc: 412 sc and 4 ch-2 sps.

Finish off White and cut Dk Pink.

CHART 2

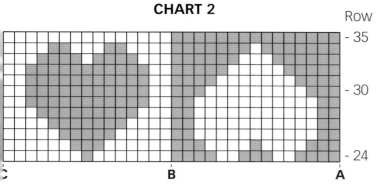

Row
- 35
- 30
- 24

C   B   A

Rnd 36: With **wrong** side facing, join Pink with dc in any corner ch-2 sp; 2 dc in same sp, ch 1, skip next 3 sc, (3 dc in next sc, ch 1, skip next 3 sc) across to next corner ch-2 sp, ★ (3 dc, ch 2, 3 dc) in corner ch-2 sp, ch 1, skip next 3 sc, (3 dc in next sc, ch 1, skip next 3 sc) across to next corner ch-2 sp; repeat from ★ around, 3 dc in same sp as first dc, hdc in first dc to form last ch-2 sp: 108 3-dc groups and 108 sps.

Rnds 37-42: Ch 3, **turn**; 2 dc in last ch-2 sp made, ch 1, (3 dc in next ch-1 sp, ch 1) across to next corner ch-2 sp, ★ (3 dc, ch 2, 3 dc) in corner ch-2 sp, ch 1, (3 dc in next ch-1 sp, ch 1) across to next corner ch-2 sp; repeat from ★ around, 3 dc in same sp as first dc, hdc in first dc to form last ch-2 sp: 132 3-dc groups and 132 sps.

Rnd 43: Ch 3, turn; 2 dc in last ch-2 sp made, ch 1, (3 dc in next ch-1 sp, ch 1) across to next corner ch-2 sp, ★ (3 dc, ch 2, 3 dc) in corner ch-2 sp, ch 1, (3 dc in next ch-1 sp, ch 1) across to next corner ch-2 sp; repeat from ★ around, 3 dc in same sp as first dc, ch 2; join with slip st to first dc, finish off: 136 3-dc groups and 136 sps.

Rnd 44: With **right** side facing, working in Back Loops Only of dc and in chs, and working over White, join Dk Pink with sc in first ch of any corner ch-2; ★ † ch 2, sc in next ch changing to White, sc in next 15 sts changing to Dk Pink in last sc made, (sc in next 15 sts changing to White in last sc made, sc in next 15 sts changing to Dk Pink in last sc made) 4 times †, sc in next ch; repeat from ★ 2 times **more**, then repeat from † to † once; join with slip st to first sc: 548 sc and 4 ch-2 sps.

Rnd 45: Ch 1, do **not** turn; working in both loops, sc in same st as joining, ★ † (sc, ch 2, sc) in next corner ch-2 sp, sc in next sc changing to White, follow Chart 2 from B to C once, then from A to C 4 times changing to Dk Pink in last sc made †, sc in next sc; repeat from ★ 2 times **more**, then repeat from † to † once; join with slip st to first sc: 556 sc and 4 ch-2 sps.

Rnd 46: Ch 1, sc in same st as joining and in next sc, ★ † (sc, ch 2, sc) in next corner ch-2 sp, sc in next 2 sc changing to White in last sc made, follow Chart 2 from B to C once, then from A to C 4 times changing to Dk Pink in last sc made †, sc in next 2 sc; repeat from ★ 2 times **more**, then repeat from † to † once; join with slip st to first sc: 564 sc and 4 ch-2 sps.

Rnd 47: Ch 1, sc in same st as joining and in next 2 sc, ★ † (2 sc, ch 2, 2 sc) in next corner ch-2 sp, sc in next 3 sc changing to White in last sc made, follow Chart 2 from B to C once, then from A to C 4 times changing to Dk Pink in last sc made †, sc in next 3 sc; repeat from ★ 2 times **more**, then repeat from † to † once; join with slip st to first sc: 580 sc and 4 ch-2 sps.

Rnds 48-56: Ch 1, sc in same st as joining and in each sc across to next corner ch-2 sp, ★ † (sc, ch 2, sc) in corner ch-2 sp, sc in each Dk Pink sc across changing to White in last sc made, follow Chart 2 from B to C once, then from A to C 4 times changing to Dk Pink in last sc made †, sc in each sc across to next corner ch-2 sp; repeat from ★ 2 times **more**, then repeat from † to † once; join with slip st to first sc: 652 sc and 4 ch-2 sps.

Finish off Dk Pink and cut White.

Rnd 57: With **wrong** side facing, join Pink with dc in any corner ch-2 sp; 2 dc in same sp, ch 1, skip next 3 sc, (3 dc in next sc, ch 1, skip next 3 sc) across to next corner ch-2 sp, ★ (3 dc, ch 2, 3 dc) in corner ch-2 sp, ch 1, skip next 3 sc, (3 dc in next sc, ch 1, skip next 3 sc) across to next corner ch-2 sp; repeat from ★ around, 3 dc in same sp as first dc, hdc in first dc to form last ch-2 sp: 168 3-dc groups and 168 sps.

Rnds 58 and 59: Ch 3, **turn**; 2 dc in last ch-2 sp made, ch 1, (3 dc in next ch-1 sp, ch 1) across to next corner ch-2 sp, ★ (3 dc, ch 2, 3 dc) in corner ch-2 sp, ch 1, (3 dc in next ch-1 sp, ch 1) across to next corner ch-2 sp; repeat from ★ around, 3 dc in same sp as first dc, ch 1, sc in first dc to form last ch-2 sp: 176 3-dc groups and 176 sps.

Rnd 60: Ch 3, turn; 4 dc in last ch-2 sp made, ch 1, (5 dc in next sp, ch 1) around; join with slip st to first dc, finish off.

Design by Annis Clapp. ●

11

big wheels

●●□□ EASY

Finished Size: 44½" x 54" (113 cm x 137 cm)

MATERIALS

Medium Weight Yarn **4 MEDIUM**
[3.5 ounces, 190 yards
(100 grams, 174 meters) per skein]:
  White - 6 skeins
  Black - 3 skeins
  Lt Grey - 2 skeins
  Med Blue - 1 skein
  Red - 1 skein
  Orange - 1 skein
  Green - 1 skein
  Blue - 1 skein
[5 ounces, 290 yards
(140 grams, 265 meters) per skein]:
  Yellow - 1 skein
Crochet hook, size H (5 mm) **or** size needed
  for gauge
Yarn needle

GAUGE SWATCH: 2½" (6.25 cm) square
Work same as Solid Square.

STITCH GUIDE

SC DECREASE
Pull up a loop in each of next 2 sc, YO and draw
through all 3 loops on hook.
HDC DECREASE (uses next 2 sts)
YO, insert hook in next st, YO and pull up a loop, pull
up a loop in next st, YO and draw through all 4 loops
on hook.

When finishing off each Square, leave end long enough
to sew two sides.

SOLID SQUARE (Make 246)

Make 120 White and 21 **each** of Med Blue, Red, Orange,
Green, Blue, and Yellow.

With color indicated, ch 4; join with slip st to form a ring.

Rnd 1: Ch 3 **(counts as first dc, now and
throughout)**, 2 dc in ring, ch 2, (3 dc in ring, ch 2) 3
times; join with slip st to first dc: 12 dc and 4 ch-2 sps.

Rnd 2 (Right side): Turn; (slip st, ch 3, 2 dc) in next
ch-2 sp, ch 1, ★ (3 dc, ch 3, 3 dc) in next ch-2 sp, ch 1;
repeat from ★ 2 times **more**, 3 dc in same sp as first
dc, ch 3; join with slip st to first dc, finish off: 24 dc and
8 sps.

Note: Loop a short piece of yarn around any stitch to
mark Rnd 2 as **right** side.

TRIANGLE SQUARE (Make 24)

Make 18 White & Lt Grey and one **each** of White &
Med Blue, White & Yellow, White & Red, White & Orange,
White & Green, and White & Blue.

Note: To change colors, drop old color and pick up new
color, YO and pull through loop on hook **(color change
ch made)**; do **not** carry yarn not in use.

With color indicated, ch 4; join with slip st to form a ring.

Rnd 1: Ch 3, (2 dc, ch 2, 3 dc) in ring, ch 1; with next
color ch 1, (3 dc in ring, ch 2) twice; join with slip st to
first dc: 12 dc and 4 ch-2 sps.

Rnd 2 (Right side): Turn; (slip st, ch 3, 2 dc) in next
ch-2 sp in same sp, ch 1, (3 dc, ch 3, 3 dc) in next
ch-2 sp, ch 1, 3 dc in next ch-2 sp, ch 2; with next color
ch 1, 3 dc in same ch-2 sp, ch 1, (3 dc, ch 3, 3 dc) in next
ch-2 sp, ch 1, 3 dc in same sp as first dc, ch 3; join with
slip st to first dc, finish off: 24 dc and 8 sps.

Note: Mark Rnd 2 as **right** side.

Instructions continued on page 14.

CIRCLE SQUARE (Make 36)

Rnd 1 (Right side): With Black, ch 2, 8 sc in second ch from hook; do **not** join, place marker to mark beginning of the rnd *(see Markers, page 91)*.

Note: Mark Rnd 1 as **right** side.

Rnd 2: 2 Sc in each sc around: 16 sc.

Rnd 3: (Sc in next sc, 2 sc in next sc) 8 times; sc in next 3 sc, slip st in next 2 sc; finish off: 24 sc.

Rnd 4: With **right** side facing and working in Back Loops Only *(Fig. 1, page 91)*, join White with hdc in any st *(see Joining With Hdc, page 91)*; sc in same st, ch 1, skip next sc, sc decrease, ch 1, skip next sc, (sc, hdc) in next sc, ch 3, ★ (hdc, sc) in next sc, ch 1, skip next sc, sc decrease, ch 1, skip next sc, (sc, hdc) in next sc, ch 3; repeat from ★ 2 times **more**; join with slip st to first hdc, finish off: 20 sts and 12 sps.

WHEEL (Make 36)

Rnd 1 (Right side): With Lt Grey, ch 2, 8 sc in second ch from hook; do **not** join, place marker to mark beginning of the rnd.

Note: Mark Rnd 1 as **right** side.

Rnd 2: 2 Sc in each sc around; sc in next sc, slip st in next sc, finish off: 16 sc.

Rnd 3: With **right** side facing, join Black with sc in any st *(see Joining With Sc, page 91)*; 2 sc in next sc, (sc in next sc, 2 sc in next sc) around; do **not** join, place marker to mark beginning of the rnd: 24 sc.

Rnd 4: (Sc in next 2 sc, 2 sc in next sc) 8 times; sc in next sc, slip st in next sc, finish off leaving a long end for sewing: 32 sc.

With Black and working through Back Loops Only, sew Wheels to Circle Squares.

BLOCK ASSEMBLY (Make 6)

With matching yarn, using Placement Diagram as a guide, and working through **inside** loops of each st on **both** pieces, whipstitch Squares together *(Fig. 10b, page 94)*, forming 18 horizontal Strips of 17 Squares each, beginning in center ch of first corner ch-3 and ending in center ch of next corner ch-3; then whipstitch 3 Strips together in same manner to form each Block.

PLACEMENT DIAGRAM

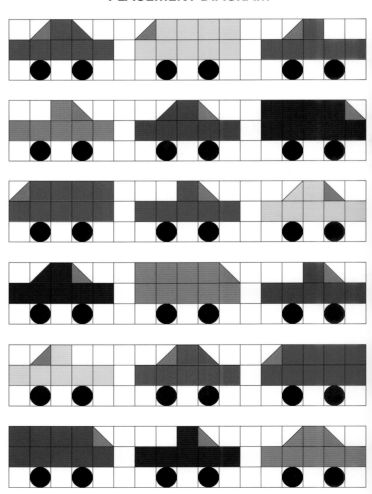

BLOCK EDGING

Rnd 1: With **right** side facing and working in Back Loops Only, join White with sc in center ch of any corner ch-3; (sc in next 9 sts, skip seam) around working (sc, ch 1, sc) in center ch of each corner ch-3, ending with sc in first center ch, ch 1; join with slip st to first sc, finish off: 368 sc and 4 ch-1 sps.

Rnd 2: With **right** side facing and working through both loops, join Black with slip st in any corner ch-1 sp; ch 3 **(counts as first hdc plus ch 1)**; ★ skip next sc, hdc in next sc, ch 1; repeat from ★ around working (hdc, ch 3, hdc) in each corner ch-1 sp and ending with hdc in first corner ch-1 sp, ch 3; join with slip st to first hdc, finish off: 190 hdc and 190 sps.

Repeat Rnds 1 and 2 around each Block Assembly, then work Row 3 on all but top Block Assembly.

Row 3: With **right** side facing and working through Back Loops Only, join Lt Grey with sc in third ch of top right corner ch-3; sc in each st across, ending with sc in first ch of top left corner ch-3, finish off: 159 sc.

FINAL ASSEMBLY

With Lt Grey, using Placement Diagram as a guide, and working through **inside** loops of Black (Rnd 2) and **both** loops of Lt Grey (Rnd 3), whipstitch Block Assemblies together.

AFGHAN EDGING

Rnd 1: With **right** side facing and working in Back Loops Only, join Lt Grey with sc in center ch of top right corner ch-3; sc in each st across top of Afghan, (sc, ch 1, sc) in center ch of next corner ch-3, sc in each st down side of Afghan including seam where Block Assembly units join and each Lt Grey row.
Repeat around entire Afghan, ending with sc in first ch, ch 1; join with slip st to first sc, finish off: 752 sc and 4 ch-1 sps.

Rnd 2: With **right** side facing and working in both loops, join Black with hdc in any corner ch-1 sp; hdc in next sc, ch 1, (hdc decrease, ch 1) around entire Afghan, working an extra hdc decrease at each corner by working in the same st twice; join with slip st to first hdc, finish off.

Design by Annis Clapp. ●

KEY

- ■ – Medium Blue Solid Square
- ■ – Yellow Solid Square
- ■ – Red Solid Square
- ■ – Orange Solid Square
- ■ – Green Solid Square
- ■ – Blue Solid Square
- □ – White Solid Square
- ● – Black & White Circle Square

- ◹ – White & Med Blue Triangle Square
- ◹ – White & Yellow Triangle Square
- ◹ – White & Red Triangle Square
- ◹ – White & Orange Triangle Square
- ◹ – White & Green Triangle Square
- ◹ – White & Blue Triangle Square
- ◹ – White & Lt Grey Triangle Square

buds & blooms

Finished Size: 38½" (98 cm) square

MATERIALS

Light Weight Yarn 🌀 **3** LIGHT
[1.75 ounces, 161 yards
(50 grams, 147 meters) per skein]:
  White - 7 skeins
  Yellow - 4 skeins
Crochet hook, size F (3.75 mm) **or** size needed
  for gauge
Safety pins - 2
Yarn needle

GAUGE: In pattern,
    17 sts **[sc, (ch 1, sc) 8 times]** = 4" (10 cm)
    One Square = 5½" (14 cm)

Gauge Swatch: 3¼" (8.25 cm) square
Work same as Square through Rnd 4.

STITCH GUIDE

POPCORN (uses one st or sp)
3 Sc in st or sp indicated, drop loop from hook,
insert hook from **front** to **back** in first sc of
3-sc group, hook dropped loop and draw through st.

SQUARE (Make 36)

With Yellow, ch 4; join with slip st to form a ring.

Rnd 1 (Right side): Ch 1, (sc in ring, ch 3) 4 times; join
with slip st to first sc: 4 sc and 4 ch-3 sps.

Note: Loop a short piece of yarn around any stitch to
mark Rnd 1 as **right** side.

Rnd 2: ★ (Slip st, ch 2, 3 dc, ch 2, slip st) in next ch-3 sp,
ch 3; repeat from ★ around; join with slip st to first
slip st, finish off: 4 Petals and 4 ch-3 sps.

Rnd 3: With **right** side facing, join White with slip st
in any ch-3 sp between Petals; ch 4 **(counts as first
dc plus ch 1, now and throughout)**, (dc, ch 1, dc)
in same sp, ch 2, ★ keeping next Petal toward you, dc
in next ch-3 sp between Petals, (ch 1, dc in same sp) 3
times, ch 2; repeat from ★ 2 times **more**, keeping next
Petal toward you, dc in same sp as joining slip st, ch 1;
join with slip st to first dc: 16 dc and 16 sps.

Rnd 4: Slip st in next corner ch-1 sp, ch 4, (dc, ch 1)
twice in same sp, (dc in next sp, ch 1) 3 times, ★ (dc,
ch 1) 4 times in next corner ch-1 sp, (dc in next sp,
ch 1) 3 times; repeat from ★ 2 times **more**, dc in same
corner ch-1 sp as first slip st, ch 1; join with slip st to first
dc, place loop from hook onto safety pin to keep piece
from unraveling as you work the next rnd: 28 dc and
28 ch-1 sps.

Keep safety pin with loop and dropped yarn on wrong
side of work throughout.

Rnd 5: With **right** side facing, join Yellow with slip st in
first corner ch-1 sp; ch 1, work (Popcorn, ch 3, Popcorn)
in same sp, ch 1, (sc in next ch-1 sp, ch 1) twice, (work
Popcorn in next ch-1 sp, ch 1) twice, (sc in next ch-1 sp,
ch 1) twice, ★ work (Popcorn, ch 3, Popcorn) in next
corner ch-1 sp, ch 1, (sc in next ch-1 sp, ch 1) twice,
(work Popcorn in next ch-1 sp, ch 1) twice, (sc in next
ch-1 sp, ch 1) twice; repeat from ★ 2 times **more**; join
with slip st to top of first Popcorn, place loop from hook
onto second safety pin to keep piece from unraveling as
you work the next rnd: 16 Popcorns and 32 sps.

Rnd 6: With **right** side facing, remove first safety pin
and, with hook **behind** sts of Rnd 5, place loop onto
hook; ch 2, (sc, ch 1) twice in first corner ch-3 sp, (sc
in next ch-1 sp, ch 1) 7 times, ★ (sc, ch 1) twice in next
corner ch-1 sp, (sc in next ch-1 sp, ch 1) 7 times; repeat
from ★ 2 times **more**; join with slip st to first sc, place
loop from hook onto first safety pin to keep piece from
unraveling as you work the next rnd: 36 ch-1 sps.

Rnd 7: With **right** side facing, remove second safety pin and, with hook **behind** sts of Rnd 6, place loop onto hook; ch 2, work (Popcorn, ch 3, Popcorn) in first corner ch-1 sp, (ch 1, sc in next ch-1 sp) 3 times, ch 2, skip next ch-1 sp, work Popcorn in next sc, ch 2, skip next ch-1 sp, (sc in next ch-1 sp, ch 1) 3 times, ★ work (Popcorn, ch 3, Popcorn) in next corner ch-1 sp, (ch 1, sc in next ch-1 sp) 3 times, ch 2, skip next ch-1 sp, work Popcorn in next sc, ch 2, skip next ch-1 sp, (sc in next ch-1 sp, ch 1) 3 times; repeat from ★ 2 times **more**; join with slip st to top of first Popcorn, finish off: 12 Popcorns and 36 sps.

Rnd 8: With **right** side facing, remove first safety pin and, with hook **behind** sts of Rnd 7, place loop onto hook; ch 2, (sc, ch 1) twice in first corner ch-3 sp, (sc in next sp, ch 1) 8 times, ★ (sc, ch 1) twice in next corner ch-1 sp, (sc in next sp, ch 1) 8 times; repeat from ★ 2 times **more**; join with slip st to first sc, do **not** finish off: 40 ch-1 sps.

Instructions continued on page 21.

candy **sprinkles**

■■■□ **INTERMEDIATE**

Finished Size: 33" x 45" (84 cm x 114.5 cm)

MATERIALS
Light Weight Yarn
[6 ounces, 490 yards
(170 grams, 448 meters) per skein]:
  White - 2 skeins
[2.5 ounces, 165 yards
(70 grams, 150 meters) per skein]:
  Orange - 2 skeins
  Purple - 2 skeins
  Green - 2 skeins
  Pink - 2 skeins
Crochet hook, size G (4 mm) **or** size needed
  for gauge
Yarn needle

GAUGE SWATCH: 3" (7.5 cm) square
Work same as Square.

STITCH GUIDE

CLUSTER (uses one ch)
Ch 3, YO, insert hook in third ch from hook, YO and pull up a loop, YO and draw through 2 loops on hook, YO, insert hook in same ch, YO and pull up a loop, YO and draw through 2 loops on hook, YO, draw through all 3 loops on hook.

SQUARE (Make 35 **each** with Orange, Purple, Green, and Pink Buttons)

BUTTON
Rnd 1 (Right side)**:** Make a slip knot on hook, lengthen loop on hook to ¼" (7 mm), ch 3, 11 hdc in third ch from hook **(2 skipped chs count as first hdc)**; join with slip st to Front Loop Only of first hdc **(Fig. 1, page 91)**: 12 hdc.

Note: Loop a short piece of yarn around any stitch to mark Rnd 1 as **right** side.

Rnd 2: Ch 3 **(counts as first dc, now and throughout)**; working in Back Loops Only **(Fig. 1, page 91)**, dc in next 11 hdc and in joining slip st; join with slip st to first dc, finish off leaving a 10" (25.5 cm) length for sewing: 13 dc.

Close Button: With **right** side facing, weave beginning strand under sts around center hole and gather tightly; secure end and clip strand close to work. Thread yarn needle with 10" (25.5 cm) length and weave strand in Front Loops Only of each dc around. Gather sts tightly; weave strand under sts around center hole and clip strand close to work.

BODY
Rnd 1: With **right** side of Rnd 2 facing and working in free loops of hdc on Button Rnd 1 **(Fig. 2a, page 91)**, join White with sc in any hdc **(see Joining With Sc, page 91)**; ch 6, sc in next hdc, ★ ch 4, skip next hdc, sc in next hdc, ch 6, sc in next hdc; repeat from ★ 2 times **more**, ch 1, dc in first sc to form last ch-4 sp: 8 sps.

Rnd 2: Ch 4 **(counts as first dc plus ch 1)**, (3 dc, ch 3, 3 dc) in next ch-6 sp, ch 1, ★ dc in next ch-4 sp, ch 1, (3 dc, ch 3, 3 dc) in next ch-6 sp, ch 1; repeat from ★ 2 times **more**; join with slip st to first dc, finish off: 28 dc and 12 sps.

Instructions continued on page 20.

continued from **candy sprinkles** page 18

ASSEMBLY

With White, using Placement Diagram as a guide, and working through **both** loops of each st on **both** pieces, whipstitch Squares together *(Fig. 10a, page 94)*, forming 10 vertical strips of 14 Squares each, beginning in center ch of first ch-3 and ending in center ch of next ch-3; then whipstitch strips together in same manner.

PLACEMENT DIAGRAM

A	B	A	B	A	B	A	B	A	B
C	D	C	D	C	D	C	D	C	D
B	A	B	A	B	A	B	A	B	A
D	C	D	C	D	C	D	C	D	C
A	B	A	B	A	B	A	B	A	B
C	D	C	D	C	D	C	D	C	D
B	A	B	A	B	A	B	A	B	A
D	C	D	C	D	C	D	C	D	C
A	B	A	B	A	B	A	B	A	B
C	D	C	D	C	D	C	D	C	D
B	A	B	A	B	A	B	A	B	A
D	C	D	C	D	C	D	C	D	C
A	B	A	B	A	B	A	B	A	B
C	D	C	D	C	D	C	D	C	D

KEY

A - Orange   B - Purple   C - Green   D - Pink

EDGING

Rnd 1: With **right** side facing, join White with sc in second ch-1 sp before top corner ch-3 sp; ch 1, sc in next ch-1 sp, ch 1, skip next dc, sc in next dc, ch 1, (sc, ch 3, sc) in corner ch-3 sp, ch 1, skip next dc, sc in next dc, ch 1, ★ † (sc in next sp, ch 1) twice, skip next dc, sc in next dc, ch 1 †; repeat from † to † across to next corner ch-3 sp, (sc, ch 3, sc) in corner ch-3 sp; repeat from ★ 2 times **more**, then repeat from † to † across; join with slip st to first sc: 288 sc.

Rnd 2: Ch 1, sc in same st, ch 1, (sc in next sc, ch 1) twice, skip next sc, (dc, ch 1, dc, ch 3, dc, ch 1, dc) in next corner ch-3 sp, ch 1, ★ skip next sc, (sc in next sc, ch 1) 4 times, [skip next sc, (dc, ch 3, dc) in next ch-1 sp, ch 1, skip next sc, (sc in next sc, ch 1) 4 times] across to within one sc of next corner ch-3 sp, skip next sc, (dc, ch 1, dc, ch 3, dc, ch 1, dc) in corner ch-3 sp, ch 1; repeat from ★ 2 times **more**, [skip next sc, (sc in next sc, ch 1) 4 times, skip next sc, (dc, ch 3, dc) in next ch-1 sp, ch 1] across to last 2 sc, skip next sc, sc in last sc, ch 1; join with slip st to first sc: 296 sts.

Rnd 3: Ch 1, (sc in next ch-1 sp, ch 1) twice, skip next ch-1 sp, (dc in next dc, ch 1) twice, (dc, ch 1) 4 times in next corner ch-3 sp, (dc in next dc, ch 1) twice, ★ skip next ch-1 sp, (sc in next ch-1 sp, ch 1) 3 times, † dc in next dc, ch 1, (dc, ch 1) 3 times in next ch-3 sp, dc in next dc, ch 1, skip next ch-1 sp, (sc in next ch-1 sp, ch 1) 3 times †; repeat from † to † across to within 2 dc of next corner ch-3 sp, (dc in next dc, ch 1) twice, (dc, ch 1) 4 times in corner ch-3 sp, (dc in next dc, ch 1) twice; repeat from ★ 2 times **more**, [skip next ch-1 sp, (sc in next ch-1 sp, ch 1) 3 times, skip next ch-1 sp, dc in next dc, ch 1, (dc, ch 1) 3 times in next ch-3 sp, dc in next dc, ch 1] across to last 2 ch-1 sps, skip next ch-1 sp, sc in last ch-1 sp, ch 1; join with slip st to first sc: 396 sts.

Rnd 4: Ch 1, sc in same st, ch 1, skip next sc, dc in next dc, (work Cluster, dc in next dc) 7 times, ch 1, ★ skip next sc, sc in next sc, † ch 1, skip next sc, dc in next dc, (work Cluster, dc in next dc) 4 times, ch 1, skip next sc, sc in next sc †; repeat from † to † across to within one sc of next corner 8-dc group, ch 1, skip next sc, dc in next dc, (work Cluster, dc in next dc) 7 times, ch 1; repeat from ★ 2 times **more**, [skip next sc, sc in next sc, ch 1, skip next sc, dc in next dc, (work Cluster, dc in next dc) 4 times, ch 1] across to last sc, skip last sc; join with slip st to first sc, finish off.

Design by Anne Halliday. ●

continued from **buds & blooms** page 17

Rnd 9: Slip st in next corner ch-1 sp, ch 1, (sc in same sp, ch 1) twice, (sc in next ch-1 sp, ch 1) 9 times, ★ (sc, ch 1) twice in next ch-1 sp, (sc in next ch-1 sp, ch 1) 9 times; repeat from ★ 2 times **more**; join with slip st to first sc, finish off: 44 ch-1 sps.

ASSEMBLY

Join Squares as follows:
With **right** side of **first Square** facing, join White with slip st in any corner ch-1 sp; ch 1, holding **second Square** with **wrong** side facing, slip st in corresponding corner ch-1 sp, ch 1, ★ slip st in next ch-1 sp on **first Square**, ch 1, slip st in next ch-1 sp on **second Square**, ch 1; repeat from ★ across to next corner ch-1 sp on **first Square**, slip st in corner ch-1 sp on **first Square**, ch 1, slip st in next corner ch-1 sp on **second Square**, ch 1, slip st in same corner sp on **first Square**; finish off.

Join Squares together forming 6 vertical strips of 6 Squares each; then join strips together in same manner.

EDGING

Rnd 1: With **right** side facing, join White with slip st in any corner ch-1 sp; ch 1, (sc in same sp, ch 1) twice, ★ (sc in next sp, ch 1) across to next corner ch-1 sp, (sc, ch 1) twice in corner ch-1 sp; repeat from ★ 2 times **more**, (sc in next sp, ch 1) across; join with slip st to first sc.

Rnd 2: Slip st in next corner ch-1 sp, ch 1, (sc in same sp, ch 1) twice, ★ (sc in next ch-1 sp, ch 1) across to next corner ch-1 sp, (sc, ch 1) twice in corner ch-1 sp; repeat from ★ 2 times **more**, (sc in next sp, ch 1) across; join with slip st to first sc, finish off.

Rnd 3: With **right** side facing, join Yellow with slip st in any corner ch-1 sp; ch 1, work (Popcorn, ch 3, Popcorn) in same sp, ch 1, ★ (sc in next ch-1 sp, ch 1) across to next corner ch-1 sp, work (Popcorn, ch 3, Popcorn) in corner ch-1 sp, ch 1; repeat from ★ 2 times **more**, (sc in next ch-1 sp, ch 1) across; join with slip st to top of first Popcorn, finish off.

Rnd 4: With **right** side facing, join White with slip st in any corner ch-3 sp; ch 1, (sc in same sp, ch 1) twice, ★ (sc in next ch-1 sp, ch 1) across to next corner ch-3 sp, (sc, ch 1) twice in corner ch-3 sp; repeat from ★ 2 times **more**, (sc in next ch-1 sp, ch 1) across; join with slip st to first sc, do **not** finish off.

Rnd 5: Slip st in next corner ch-1 sp, ch 1, (sc in same sp, ch 1) twice, ★ (sc in next ch-1 sp, ch 1) across to next corner ch-1 sp, (sc, ch 1) twice in corner ch-1 sp; repeat from ★ 2 times **more**, (sc in next ch-1 sp, ch 1) across; join with slip st to first sc, finish off.

Rnd 6: With **right** side facing, join Yellow with slip st in any corner ch-1 sp; ch 1, work (Popcorn, ch 3, Popcorn) in same sp, ch 1, ★ (sc in next ch-1 sp, ch 1) across to next corner ch-1 sp, work (Popcorn, ch 3, Popcorn) in corner ch-1 sp, ch 1; repeat from ★ 2 times **more**, (sc in next ch-1 sp, ch 1) across; join with slip st to top of first Popcorn, finish off.

Rnd 7: With **right** side facing, join White with slip st in any corner ch-3 sp; ch 1, (sc in same sp, ch 1) twice, ★ (sc in next ch-1 sp, ch 1) across to next corner ch-3 sp, (sc, ch 1) twice in corner ch-3 sp; repeat from ★ 2 times **more**, (sc in next ch-1 sp, ch 1) across; join with slip st to first sc, do **not** finish off.

Rnd 8: Slip st in next corner ch-1 sp, ch 1, (sc in same sp, ch 1) twice, ★ (sc in next ch-1 sp, ch 1) across to next corner ch-1 sp, (sc, ch 1) twice in corner ch-1 sp; repeat from ★ 2 times **more**, (sc in next ch-1 sp, ch 1) across; join with slip st to first sc.

Rnd 9: ★ Slip st in next ch-1 sp, ch 2, slip st in back ridge of second ch from hook *(Fig. 3a, page 92)*; repeat from ★ around; join with slip st to first slip st, finish off.

Design by Mary Ann Sipes. •

cherished reminder

■■□□ EASY +

Finished Size: 33½" x 41" (85 cm x 104 cm)

MATERIALS
Light Weight Yarn **LIGHT 3**
[7 ounces, 575 yards
(198 grams, 525 meters) per skein]:
    2 skeins
Crochet hook, size G (4 mm) **or** size needed
    for gauge

GAUGE: In pattern,
        (2 dc, ch 2, 2 dc) 4 times = 4½" (11.5 cm)
        and 8 rows = 4" (10 cm)

Gauge Swatch: 5"w x 4"h (12.75 cm x 10 cm)
Ch 21.
Work same as Afghan Body Rows 1-8.
Finish off.

STITCH GUIDE

PICOT
Ch 3, slip st in top of last dc made **(Fig. 7, page 93)**.

AFGHAN BODY
Ch 141; place marker in third ch from hook for Edging placement.

Row 1: Sc in second ch from hook and in next ch, ★ ch 4, skip next 4 chs, sc in next 2 chs; repeat from ★ across: 23 ch-4 sps.

Row 2 (Right side)**:** Ch 3 **(counts as first dc, now and throughout)**, turn; (2 dc, ch 2, 2 dc) in each ch-4 sp across to last 2 sc, skip next sc, dc in last sc.

Note: Loop a short piece of yarn around any stitch to mark Row 2 as **right** side.

Row 3: Ch 5 **(counts as first dc plus ch 2, now and throughout)**, turn; 2 sc in next ch-2 sp, (ch 4, 2 sc in next ch-2 sp) across, ch 2, skip next 2 dc, dc in last dc: 24 sps.

Row 4: Ch 4 **(counts as first dc plus ch 1, now and throughout)**, turn; 2 dc in next ch-2 sp, (2 dc, ch 2, 2 dc) in each ch-4 sp across to last ch-2 sp, 2 dc in last ch-2 sp, ch 1, dc in last dc.

Row 5: Ch 1, turn; sc in first dc and in next ch-1 sp, ch 4, (2 sc in next ch-2 sp, ch 4) across to last ch-1 sp, sc in last ch-1 sp and in last dc: 23 ch-4 sps.

Row 6: Ch 3, turn; (2 dc, ch 2, 2 dc) in each ch-4 sp across to last 2 sc, skip next sc, dc in last sc.

Row 7: Ch 5, turn; 2 dc in next ch-2 sp, (ch 4, 2 dc in next ch-2 sp) across to last 3 dc, ch 2, skip next 2 dc, dc in last dc: 24 sps.

Row 8: Ch 4, turn; 2 dc in first ch-2 sp, (2 dc, ch 2, 2 dc) in each ch-4 sp across to last ch-2 sp, 2 dc in last ch-2 sp, ch 1, dc in last dc.

Row 9: Ch 1, turn; sc in first dc and in next ch-1 sp, ch 4, (2 sc in next ch-2 sp, ch 4) across to last ch-1 sp, sc in last ch-1 sp and in last dc: 23 ch-4 sps.

Row 10: Ch 3, turn; (2 dc, ch 2, 2 dc) in each ch-4 sp across to last 2 sc, skip next sc, dc in last sc.

Rows 11-68: Repeat Rows 3-10, 7 times; then repeat Rows 3 and 4 once **more**.

Finish off.

Instructions continued on page 27.

heirloom ruffles

Finished Size: 34¼" x 44¼" (87 cm x 112.5 cm)

MATERIALS

Light Weight Yarn
[7 ounces, 575 yards
(198 grams, 525 meters) per skein]:
  3 skeins
Crochet hook, size G (4 mm) **or** size needed
  for gauge

GAUGE: In pattern, (Shell, dc) 3 times = 4" (10 cm)
and 7 rows = 3¾" (9.5 cm)

Gauge Swatch: 4¼"w x 3¾"h (10.75 cm x 9.5 cm)
Ch 21.
Work same as Afghan Body Rows 1-7.
Finish off.

STITCH GUIDE

SHELL
(2 Dc, ch 2, 2 dc) in st or sp indicated.
CLUSTER (uses next 2 ch-3 sps)
★ YO, insert hook in **next** ch-3 sp, YO and pull up a
loop, YO and draw through 2 loops on hook; repeat
from ★ once **more**, YO and draw through all 3 loops
on hook.
FRONT POST SINGLE CROCHET
  (abbreviated FPsc)
Insert hook from **front** to **back** around post of st
indicated **(Fig. 6, page 93)**, YO and pull up a loop,
YO and draw through both loops on hook.
BACK POST DOUBLE CROCHET
  (abbreviated BPdc)
YO, insert hook from **back** to **front** around post of
st indicated **(Fig. 6, page 93)**, YO and pull up a loop
(3 loops on hook), (YO and draw through 2 loops on
hook) twice.
FRONT POST DOUBLE CROCHET
  (abbreviated FPdc)
YO, insert hook from **front** to **back** around post of
st indicated **(Fig. 6, page 93)**, YO and pull up a loop
(3 loops on hook), (YO and draw through 2 loops on
hook) twice.
PICOT
Ch 3, slip st in third ch from hook.

AFGHAN BODY

Ch 111; place marker in third ch from hook for st
placement.

Row 1: Work Shell in sixth ch from hook, skip next
2 chs, dc in next ch, ★ skip next 2 chs, work Shell in next
ch, skip next 2 chs, dc in next ch; repeat from ★ across:
18 Shells.

Row 2 (Right side): Ch 3 **(counts as first dc, now and
throughout)**, turn; ★ work Shell in next ch-2 sp, skip
next 2 dc, dc in next st; repeat from ★ across.

Instructions continued on page 26.

continued from **heirloom ruffles** page 24

Rows 3-64: Ch 3, turn; ★ work Shell in next ch-2 sp, skip next 2 dc, dc in next dc; repeat from ★ across; at end of Row 64, do **not** finish off.

EDGING

Rnd 1: Ch 1, do **not** turn; 2 sc in last dc made on Row 64; work 157 sc evenly spaced across end of rows; working in free loops of beginning ch *(Fig. 2b, page 91)*, 3 sc in marked ch, 2 sc in next ch, sc in each ch across to last 2 chs, 2 sc in next ch, 3 sc in last ch; work 157 sc evenly spaced across end of rows; 3 sc in first dc on Row 64, 2 sc in next dc, sc in next dc and in next ch-2 sp, (sc in next 5 sts, sc in next ch-2 sp) across to last 2 dc, sc in next dc, 2 sc in last dc, sc in same st as first sc; join with slip st to first sc: 544 sc.

Rnd 2: Ch 4 **(counts as first dc plus ch 1)**, (dc in same st, ch 1) twice, skip next sc, (dc in next sc, ch 1, skip next sc) across to center sc of next corner 3-sc group, ★ (dc, ch 1) 3 times in center sc, skip next sc, (dc in next sc, ch 1, skip next sc) across to center sc of next corner 3-sc group; repeat from ★ around; join with slip st to first dc: 280 ch-1 sps.

Rnd 3: Slip st in next ch-1 sp, ch 1, (sc, ch 3) twice in same sp, † place marker around last ch-3 made to mark corner, (sc, ch 3, sc) in each of next 81 ch-1 sps, (sc, ch 3) twice in next ch-1 sp, place marker around last ch-3 made to mark corner, (sc, ch 3, sc) in each of next 57 ch-1 sps †, (sc, ch 3) twice in next ch-1 sp, repeat from † to † once; join with slip st to first sc: 284 ch-3 sps.

Rnds 4 and 5: Slip st in next ch-3 sp, ch 1, (sc, ch 3, sc) in same sp and in each ch-3 sp around, moving each corner marker from rnd below to corner ch-3 just made; join with slip st to first sc.

Rnd 6: (Slip st, ch 1, sc, ch 3, sc) in next ch-3 sp, (sc, ch 3) twice in marked ch-3 sp, move marker to corner ch-3 just made, ★ (sc, ch 3, sc) in same sp and in each ch-3 sp across to next marked ch-3 sp, (sc, ch 3) twice in marked ch-3 sp, move marker to corner ch-3 just made; repeat from ★ 2 times **more**, (sc, ch 3, sc) in same sp and in each ch-3 sp across; join with slip st to first sc: 292 ch-3 sps.

Rnds 7 and 8: Slip st in next ch-3 sp, ch 1, (sc, ch 3, sc) in same sp and in each ch-3 sp around, moving each corner marker from rnd below to corner ch-3 just made; join with slip st to first sc.

Rnd 9: Slip st in next ch-3 sp, ch 1, (sc, ch 3, sc) in same sp and in next ch-3 sp, (sc, ch 3) twice in marked ch-3 sp, move marker to corner ch-3 just made, ★ (sc, ch 3, sc) in same sp and in each ch-3 sp across to next marked ch-3 sp, (sc, ch 3) twice in marked ch-3 sp, move marker to corner ch-3 just made; repeat from ★ 2 times **more**, (sc, ch 3, sc) in same sp and in each ch-3 sp across; join with slip st to first sc: 300 ch-3 sps.

Rnds 10 and 11: Slip st in next ch-3 sp, ch 1, (sc, ch 3, sc) in same sp and in each ch-3 sp around, moving each corner marker from rnd below to corner ch-3 just made; join with slip st to first sc.

Rnd 12: (Slip st, ch 3, dc, ch 2, 2 dc) in next ch-3 sp, (dc in next ch-3 sp, work Shell in next ch-3 sp) 3 times, ★ (work Cluster, work Shell in next ch-3 sp) across to within 2 ch-3 sps of next corner ch-3 sp, (dc in next ch-3 sp, work Shell in next ch-3 sp) 3 times; repeat from ★ 2 times **more**, work Cluster, (work Shell in next ch-3 sp, work Cluster) across; join with slip st to first dc.

Rnd 13: Ch 3, work BPdc around next dc, work Shell in next ch-2 sp, work BPdc around each of next 2 dc, work FPdc around next st, ★ work BPdc around each of next 2 dc, work Shell in next ch-2 sp, work BPdc around each of next 2 dc, work FPdc around next st; repeat from ★ around; join with slip st to first dc.

Rnd 14: Slip st in next BPdc, ch 1, sc in same st and in next 2 dc, (sc, work Picot, sc) in next ch-2 sp, sc in next 3 sts, skip next BPdc, work FPsc around next FPdc, skip next BPdc, ★ sc in next 3 sts, (sc, work Picot, sc) in next ch-2 sp, sc in next 3 sts, skip next BPdc, work FPsc around next FPdc, skip next st; repeat from ★ around; join with slip st to first sc, finish off.

Design by Kay Meadors. ●

EDGING

Foundation Row: With **wrong** side facing and working in free loops of beginning ch *(Fig. 2b, page 91)*, join yarn with slip st in marked ch; (sc, ch 4) twice in next ch; working in end of rows, skip first sc row, sc around next dc, ch 4, sc in top of next dc, ch 4, (skip next 2 rows, sc around next dc, ch 4, sc in top of next dc, ch 4) across to last dc row, skip last dc row; (sc, ch 4, sc) in first dc on Row 68, sc in next ch-1 sp, ch 4, (2 sc in next ch-2 sp, ch 4) across to last ch-1 sp, sc in last ch-1 sp, (sc, ch 4, sc) in last dc, place marker around last ch-4 made for st placement, ch 4; working in end of rows, skip first dc row, sc in top of next dc, ch 4, sc around next dc, ch 4, (skip next 2 rows, sc in top of next dc, ch 4, sc around next dc, ch 4) across to last sc row, skip last sc row; working in free loops of beginning ch, (sc, ch 4, sc) in first ch, slip st in next ch; finish off leaving remaining 23 ch-4 sps across beginning ch unworked: 120 ch-4 sps around entire Afghan Body.

Rnd 1: With **right** side facing, join yarn with slip st in marked ch-4 sp; ch 3, dc in same sp, (ch 2, 2 dc in same sp) twice, 3 sc in next ch-4 sp, **[**(2 dc, ch 2, 2 dc) in next ch-4 sp, 3 sc in next ch-4 sp**]** across to next corner ch-4 sp, ★ 2 dc in corner ch-4 sp, (ch 2, 2 dc in same sp) twice, 3 sc in next ch-4 sp, **[**(2 dc, ch 2, 2 dc) in next ch-4 sp, 3 sc in next ch-4 sp**]** across to next corner ch-4 sp; repeat from ★ 2 times **more**; join with slip st to first dc: 64 ch-2 sps.

Rnd 2: Slip st in next dc and in next ch-2 sp, ch 3, (dc, ch 2, 2 dc) in same sp, ch 5, ★ (2 dc, ch 2, 2 dc) in next ch-2 sp, ch 5; repeat from ★ around; join with slip st to first dc: 128 sps.

Rnd 3: Slip st in next dc and in next ch-2 sp, ch 3, (2 dc, ch 2, 3 dc) in same sp, ch 4, skip next ch-5 sp, ★ (3 dc, ch 2, 3 dc) in next ch-2 sp, ch 4, skip next ch-5 sp; repeat from ★ around; join with slip st to first dc.

Rnd 4: Slip st in next 2 dc and in next ch-2 sp, ch 3, (2 dc, ch 3, 3 dc) in same sp, ch 3, working **around** next ch-4 *(Fig. 9, page 93)*, sc in next ch-5 sp on Rnd 2, ch 3, ★ (3 dc, ch 3, 3 dc) in next ch-2 sp, ch 3, working **around** next ch-4, sc in next ch-5 sp on Rnd 2, ch 3; repeat from ★ around; join with slip st to first dc: 192 ch-3 sps.

Rnd 5: Slip st in next 2 dc and in next ch-3 sp, ch 6, slip st in fourth ch from hook, ch 1, dc in same sp, (work Picot, ch 1, dc in same sp) 4 times, skip next ch-3 sp, (dc, ch 1, dc) in next sc, skip next ch-3 sp, ★ dc in next ch-3 sp, (work Picot, ch 1, dc in same sp) 5 times, skip next ch-3 sp, (dc, ch 1, dc) in next sc, skip next ch-3 sp; repeat from ★ around; join with slip st to third ch of beginning ch-6, finish off.

Design by Kay Meadors. ●

hugs & hearts

Finished Size: 33" x 42" (84 cm x 106.5 cm)

MATERIALS

Light Weight Yarn **③ LIGHT**
[1.75 ounces, 180 yards
(50 grams, 165 meters) per skein]:
  White - 8 skeins
  Green - 4 skeins
  Pink - 2 skeins
Crochet hook, size G (4 mm) **or** size needed
  for gauge

GAUGE: In pattern,
  (sc, ch 1) 9 times = 4¼" (10.75 cm);
  Rows 1-14 = 4" (10 cm)

Gauge Swatch: 4" (10 cm) square
With White, ch 18.
Row 1 (Right side): Sc in second ch from hook, ★ ch 1, skip next ch, sc in next ch; repeat from ★ across; finish off: 9 sc.
Note: Mark Row 1 as **right** side.
Row 2: With **wrong** side facing, join Green with sc in first sc **(see Joining With Sc, page 91)**; (ch 1, sc in next sc) across; finish off.
Row 3: With **right** side facing, join White with sc in first sc; (ch 1, sc in next sc) across; finish off.
Rows 4-16: Repeat Rows 2 and 3, 6 times; then repeat Row 2 once **more**.

> Each row is worked across length of Afghan. When joining and finishing off, leave an 8" (20.5 cm) length to be worked into fringe.

STITCH GUIDE

STITCH GUIDE

CLUSTER
YO, insert hook in Back Loop Only of ch indicated **(Fig. 1, page 91)**, YO and pull up a loop, YO and draw through 2 loops on hook, YO, insert hook in same st, YO and pull up a loop, YO and draw through 2 loops on hook, YO and draw through all 3 loops on hook. Push Cluster to **right** side.

AFGHAN BODY

With White, ch 182; place marker in fourth ch from hook for st placement.

Row 1 (Right side): Dc in sixth ch from hook, ★ ch 1, skip next ch, dc in next ch; repeat from ★ across: 90 sts and 89 sps.

Note: Loop a short piece of yarn around any stitch to mark Row 1 as **right** side.

Row 2: Ch 1, turn; sc in first dc, ★ work Cluster in next ch, sc in next dc, ch 1, skip next ch, sc in next dc; repeat from ★ across to last sp, work Cluster in next ch, sc in next ch: 179 sts.

Row 3: Ch 4 **(counts as first dc plus ch 1, now and throughout)**, turn; skip next Cluster, dc in next sc, ★ ch 1, skip next st, dc in next sc; repeat from ★ across; finish off: 90 dc and 89 ch-1 sps.

Row 4: With **wrong** side facing, join Green with sc in first dc **(see Joining With Sc, page 91)**; ★ ch 1, skip next ch, sc in next dc; repeat from ★ across; finish off.

Row 5: With **right** side facing, join White with sc in first sc; ★ ch 1, skip next ch, sc in next sc; repeat from ★ across; finish off.

Rows 6 and 7: Repeat Rows 4 and 5.

Instructions continued on page 33.

lemon drop

■■■□ INTERMEDIATE

Finished Size: 39" x 51" (99 cm x 129.5 cm)

MATERIALS

Medium Weight Yarn **4**
[3.5 ounces, 216 yards
(100 grams, 197 meters) per skein]:
   White - 5 skeins
   Yellow - 4 skeins
Crochet hook, size I (5.5 mm) **or** size needed
   for gauge
Yarn needle

GAUGE: Each Strip - 4" (10 cm) wide

Gauge Swatch: 3"w x 7"h (7.5 cm x 17.75 cm)
Foundation: With White, ch 3, dc in third ch from hook,
ch 14, dc in third ch from hook: 2 rings.
Rnd 1 (Right side): Ch 5, working across dc side of ring,
(tr, ch 1) 6 times in first ring, † skip next 3 chs, sc in
next ch, ch 1, (skip next ch, sc in next ch, ch 1) twice †,
(tr, ch 1) 12 times in last ring; working in free loops of
Foundation chs **(Fig. 2b, page 91)** and across ch-3 side
of rings, repeat from † to † once, (tr, ch 1) 5 times in
same ring as beginning ch-5; join with slip st to fourth ch
of beginning ch-5: 30 sts and 30 ch-1 sps.
Rnd 2: Ch 1, turn; sc in same st, ch 1, skip next ch, ★ sc
in next st, ch 1, skip next ch; repeat from ★ around; join
with slip st to first sc, finish off.

STITCH GUIDE

TREBLE CROCHET (abbreviated tr)
YO twice, insert hook in sp indicated, YO and pull
up a loop (4 loops on hook), (YO and draw through
2 loops on hook) 3 times.

DECREASE (uses next 3 dc)
YO, † insert hook in **next** dc, YO and pull up a loop,
YO and draw through 2 loops on hook †, YO, skip
next dc, repeat from † to † once, YO and draw
through all 3 loops on hook.

LEFT DECREASE
YO, insert hook in next dc, YO and pull up a loop, YO
and draw through 2 loops on hook, skip next joining,
★ YO, insert hook in **next** dc, YO and pull up a loop,
YO and draw through 2 loops on hook; repeat from
★ once **more**, YO and draw through all 4 loops on
hook.

RIGHT DECREASE
★ YO, insert hook in **next** dc, YO and pull up a loop,
YO and draw through 2 loops on hook; repeat from
★ once **more**, YO, skip next joining, insert hook in
next dc, YO and pull up a loop, YO and draw through
2 loops on hook, YO and draw through all 4 loops on
hook.

STRIP A (Make 6)

Foundation: With White, ch 3, dc in third ch from hook,
(ch 14, dc in third ch from hook) 12 times: 13 rings.

Rnd 1 (Right side): Ch 5, working across dc side of rings,
(tr, ch 1) 6 times in first ring, † skip next 3 chs, sc in next
ch, ch 1, (skip next ch, sc in next ch, ch 1) twice, [(tr,
ch 1) 5 times in next ring, skip next 3 chs, sc in next ch,
ch 1, (skip next ch, sc in next ch, ch 1) twice] 11 times †,
(tr, ch 1) 12 times in last ring; working in free loops of
Foundation chs **(Fig. 2b, page 91)** and across ch-3
side of rings, repeat from † to † once, (tr, ch 1) 5 times in
same ring as beginning ch-5; join with slip st to fourth ch
of beginning ch-5: 206 sts and 206 ch-1 sps.

Note: Loop a short piece of yarn around any stitch to
mark Rnd 1 as **right** side.

Rnd 2: Ch 1, turn; sc in same st, ch 1, skip next ch, ★ sc in next st, ch 1, skip next ch; repeat from ★ around; join with slip st to first sc, finish off.

Rnd 3: With **right** side facing, join Yellow with slip st in same st as joining; ch 4 **(counts as first dc plus ch 1, now and throughout)**, dc in same st, (ch 1, dc) twice in each of next 4 sc, † place marker around last ch-1 made for joining placement, ch 1, (dc in next sc, ch 1) twice, dc in next 3 sc, (ch 1, dc in next sc) twice, **[**(ch 1, dc) twice in next sc, ch 1, (dc in next sc, ch 1) twice, dc in next 3 sc, (ch 1, dc in next sc) twice**]** 11 times, (ch 1, dc) twice in next sc, place marker around last ch-1 made for joining placement †, (ch 1, dc) twice in each of next 7 sc, repeat from † to † once, ch 1, (dc, ch 1) twice in each of last 2 sc; join with slip st to first dc, finish off: 244 dc and 196 ch-1 sps.

STRIP B (Make 5)

Foundation: With White, ch 3, dc in third ch from hook, (ch 14, dc in third ch from hook) 11 times: 12 rings.

Rnd 1 (Right side)**:** Ch 5, working across dc side of rings, (tr, ch 1) 6 times in first ring, † skip next 3 chs, sc in next ch, ch 1, (skip next ch, sc in next ch, ch 1) twice, **[**(tr, ch 1) 5 times in next ring, skip next 3 chs, sc in next ch, ch 1, (skip next ch, sc in next ch, ch 1) twice**]** 10 times †, (tr, ch 1) 12 times in last ring; working in free loops of Foundation chs and across ch-3 side of rings, repeat from † to † once, (tr, ch 1) 5 times in same ring as beginning ch-5; join with slip st to fourth ch of beginning ch-5: 190 sts and 190 ch-1 sps.

Instructions continued on page 32.

Note: Mark Rnd 1 as **right** side.

Rnd 2: Ch 1, turn; sc in same st, ch 1, skip next ch, ★ sc in next st, ch 1, skip next ch; repeat from ★ around; join with slip st to first sc, finish off.

Rnd 3: With **right** side facing, join Yellow with slip st in same st as joining; ch 4, dc in same st, (ch 1, dc) twice in each of next 2 sc, place marker around last ch-1 made for joining placement, † (ch 1, dc) twice in each of next 2 sc, ch 1, (dc in next sc, ch 1) twice, dc in next 3 sc, (ch 1, dc in next sc) twice, [(ch 1, dc) twice in next sc, ch 1, (dc in next sc, ch 1) twice, dc in next 3 sc, (ch 1, dc in next sc) twice] 10 times †, [(ch 1, dc) twice in each of next 3 sc, place marker around last ch-1 made for joining placement] twice, repeat from † to † once, (ch 1, dc) twice in each of next 3 sc, place marker around last ch-1 made for joining placement, ch 1; join with slip st to first dc, finish off: 226 dc and 182 ch-1 sps.

ASSEMBLY

With Yellow and working through **both** loops of each stitch on **both** pieces, whipstitch long edges of Strips together **(Fig. 10a, page 94)**, beginning in first marked ch-1 and ending in next marked ch-1 in the following sequence: Strip A, (Strip B, Strip A) 5 times. Leave markers in place on outer Strips.

EDGING

Rnd 1: With **right** side facing, join Yellow with slip st in marked ch-1 sp at top right corner; ch 4, dc in next dc, (ch 1, dc in next dc) 12 times, † work left decrease, dc in next dc, ch 1, dc in next ch-1 sp, ch 1, dc in next dc, work right decrease, [dc in next dc, (ch 1, dc in next dc) 11 times, work left decrease, dc in next dc, ch 1, dc in next ch-1 sp, ch 1, dc in next dc, work right decrease] 4 times, (dc in next dc, ch 1) 13 times, [dc in next ch-1 sp, (ch 1, dc in next dc) 3 times, decrease, (dc in next dc, ch 1) 3 times] 12 times †, dc in next ch-1 sp, (ch 1, dc in next dc) 13 times, repeat from † to † once; join with slip st to first dc: 392 sts and 304 ch-1 sps.

Rnd 2: Slip st in next ch-1 sp, (ch 2, slip st in next ch-1 sp) 12 times, † skip next dc, slip st in next st, skip next dc, slip st in next ch-1 sp, ch 2, slip st in next ch-1 sp, skip next dc, slip st in next st, skip next dc, slip st in next ch-1 sp, [(ch 2, slip st in next ch-1 sp) 10 times, skip next dc, slip st in next st, skip next dc, slip st in next ch-1 sp, ch 2, slip st in next ch-1 sp, skip next dc, slip st in next st, skip next dc, slip st in next ch-1 sp] 4 times, (ch 2, slip st in next ch-1 sp) 15 times, skip next dc, slip st in next st, skip next dc, slip st in next ch-1 sp, [(ch 2, slip st in next ch-1 sp) 5 times, skip next dc, slip st in next st, skip next dc, slip st in next ch-1 sp] 11 times †, (ch 2, slip st in next ch-1 sp) 15 times, repeat from † to † once, ch 2, (slip st in next ch-1 sp, ch 2) twice; join with slip st to first slip st, finish off.

Design by Anne Halliday. ●

Row 8: With **wrong** side facing, join Green with sc in first sc; (ch 1, skip next ch, sc in next sc) twice, (work Cluster in next ch, sc in next sc) 3 times, ★ (ch 1, skip next ch, sc in next sc) 7 times, (work Cluster in next ch, sc in next sc) 3 times; repeat from ★ across to last 4 sc, (ch 1, skip next ch, sc in next sc) 4 times; finish off: 90 sc, 27 Clusters, and 62 ch-1 sps.

Row 9: With **right** side facing, join White with sc in first sc; ★ ch 1, skip next st, sc in next sc; repeat from ★ across; finish off: 90 sc and 89 ch-1 sps.

Row 10: With **wrong** side facing, join Green with sc in first sc; ch 1, skip next ch, sc in next sc, (work Cluster in next ch, sc in next sc) 5 times, ★ (ch 1, skip next ch, sc in next sc) 5 times, (work Cluster in next ch, sc in next sc) 5 times; repeat from ★ across to last 3 sc, (ch 1, skip next ch, sc in next sc) 3 times; finish off: 90 sc, 45 Clusters, and 44 ch-1 sps.

Row 11: Repeat Row 9.

Row 12: With **wrong** side facing, join Green with sc in first sc; ch 1, skip next ch, sc in next sc, (work Cluster in next ch, sc in next sc) 6 times, ★ (ch 1, skip next ch, sc in next sc) 4 times, (work Cluster in next ch, sc in next sc) 6 times; repeat from ★ across to last 2 sc, (ch 1, skip next ch, sc in next sc) twice; finish off: 90 sc, 54 Clusters, and 35 ch-1 sps.

Row 13: Repeat Row 9.

Row 14: With **wrong** side facing, join Green with sc in first sc; (ch 1, skip next ch, sc in next sc) twice, (work Cluster in next ch, sc in next sc) 6 times, ★ (ch 1, skip next ch, sc in next sc) 4 times, (work Cluster in next ch, sc in next sc) 6 times; repeat from ★ across to last sc, ch 1, skip next ch, sc in last sc; finish off: 90 sc, 54 Clusters, and 35 ch-1 sps.

Row 15: Repeat Row 9.

Row 16: Repeat Row 12.

Rows 17-19: Repeat Rows 9 and 10 once, then repeat Row 9 once **more**.

Row 20: Repeat Row 8.

Row 21: With **right** side facing, join White with sc in first sc; ★ ch 1, skip next st, sc in next sc; repeat from ★ across; finish off: 90 sc and 89 ch-1 sps.

Row 22: With **wrong** side facing, join Green with sc in first sc; ★ ch 1, skip next ch, sc in next sc; repeat from ★ across; finish off.

Rows 23 and 24: Repeat Rows 21 and 22.

Row 25: With **right** side facing, join White with dc in first sc *(see Joining With Dc, page 91)*; ★ ch 1, skip next ch, dc in next sc; repeat from ★ across; do **not** finish off.

Rows 26 and 27: Repeat Rows 2 and 3: 90 dc and 89 ch-1 sps.

Row 28: With **wrong** side facing, join Pink with sc in first dc; ★ ch 1, skip next ch, sc in next dc; repeat from ★ across; finish off.

Rows 29-51: Repeat Rows 5-27 replacing Pink with Green.

Rows 52-123: Repeat Rows 4-51 once, then repeat Rows 4-27 once **more**.

TRIM
FIRST SIDE
With **right** side facing, join White with slip st in first dc; slip st in next ch-1 sp, (ch 1, slip st in next ch-1 sp) across to last dc, slip st in last dc; finish off.

SECOND SIDE
With **right** side facing and working in sps and in free loops of beginning ch *(Fig. 2b, page 91)*, join White with slip st in first ch; slip st in next sp, (ch 1, slip st in next sp) across to marked ch, slip st in marked ch; finish off.

Holding 5 strands of White yarn together, each 18" (45.5 cm) long, add additional fringe across short edges of Afghan Body *(Figs. 11a & b, page 94)*.

Design by Anne Halliday. ●

lacy treasure

■■■▢ INTERMEDIATE

Finished Size: 35½" x 46½" (90 cm x 118 cm)

MATERIALS
Light Weight Yarn **③**
[7 ounces, 575 yards
(198 grams, 525 meters) per skein]:
   3 skeins
Crochet hook, size G (4 mm) **or** size needed
   for gauge

GAUGE: In pattern, 18 sts and 8 rows = 4" (10 cm)

Gauge Swatch: 4¼"w x 4"h (10.75 cm x 10 cm)
Ch 21.
Work same as Afghan Body Rows 1-8.
Finish off.

STITCH GUIDE

CLUSTER (uses one ch-5 sp)
★ YO, insert hook in ch-5 sp indicated, YO and pull
up a loop, YO and draw through 2 loops on hook;
repeat from ★ once **more**, YO and draw through all
3 loops on hook.
PICOT
Ch 3, slip st in top of last sc made **(Fig. 7, page 93)**.

AFGHAN BODY

Ch 117; place marker in third ch from hook for
st placement.

Row 1 (Right side)**:** Dc in fourth ch from hook
(3 skipped chs count as first dc) and in next ch,
★ ch 1, skip next ch, dc in next 3 chs; repeat from ★
across: 87 dc and 28 ch-1 sps.

Row 2: Ch 4 **(counts as first dc plus ch 1, now and throughout)**, turn; skip next dc, dc in next dc, ★ dc in next ch-1 sp and in next dc, ch 1, skip next dc, dc in next dc; repeat from ★ across: 86 dc and 29 ch-1 sps.

Row 3: Ch 3 **(counts as first dc, now and throughout)**, turn; dc in next ch-1 sp and in next dc, ★ ch 1, skip next dc, dc in next dc, dc in next ch-1 sp and in next dc; repeat from ★ across: 87 dc and 28 ch-1 sps.

Rows 4-17: Repeat Rows 2 and 3, 7 times.

Row 18: Ch 4, turn; † skip next dc, dc in next dc, dc in next ch-1 sp and in next dc, (ch 1, skip next dc, dc in next dc, dc in next ch-1 sp and in next dc) 5 times †, ch 4, ★ skip next dc, dc in next dc, dc in next ch-1 sp and in next dc, (ch 1, skip next dc, dc in next dc, dc in next ch-1 sp and in next dc) 3 times, ch 4; repeat from ★ 3 times **more**, then repeat from † to † once, ch 1, skip next dc, dc in last dc: 86 dc and 29 sps.

Row 19: Ch 3, turn; dc in next ch-1 sp and in next dc, (ch 1, skip next dc, dc in next dc, dc in next ch-1 sp and in next dc) 5 times, ch 5, sc in next ch-4 sp, ch 5, skip next 2 dc, dc in next dc, dc in next ch-1 sp and in next dc, ★ (ch 1, skip next dc, dc in next dc, dc in next ch-1 sp and in next dc) twice, ch 5, sc in next ch-4 sp, ch 5, skip next 2 dc, dc in next dc, dc in next ch-1 sp and in next dc; repeat from ★ 3 times **more**, (ch 1, skip next dc, dc in next dc, dc in next ch-1 sp and in next dc) across: 72 dc, 5 sc, and 28 sps.

Row 20: Ch 4, turn; skip next dc, dc in next dc, dc in next ch-1 sp and in next dc, (ch 1, skip next dc, dc in next dc, dc in next ch-1 sp and in next dc) 4 times, ch 5, sc in next ch-5 sp, sc in next sc and in next ch-5 sp, ch 5, skip next 2 dc, dc in next dc, ★ dc in next ch-1 sp and in next dc, ch 1, skip next dc, dc in next dc, dc in next ch-1 sp and in next dc, ch 5, sc in next ch-5 sp, sc in next sc and in next ch-5 sp, ch 5, skip next 2 dc, dc in next dc; repeat from ★ 3 times **more**, (dc in next ch-1 sp and in next dc, ch 1, skip next dc, dc in next dc) across: 56 dc, 15 sc, and 24 sps.

Instructions continued on page 36.

Row 21: Ch 3, turn; dc in next ch-1 sp and in next dc, (ch 1, skip next dc, dc in next dc, dc in next ch-1 sp and in next dc) 4 times, ★ ch 5, sc in next ch-5 sp, sc in next 3 sc and in next ch-5 sp, ch 5, skip next 2 dc, dc in next dc, dc in next ch-1 sp and in next dc; repeat from ★ 4 times **more**, (ch 1, skip next dc, dc in next dc, dc in next ch-1 sp and in next dc) across: 42 dc, 25 sc, and 18 sps.

Row 22: Ch 4, turn; skip next dc, dc in next dc, (dc in next ch-1 sp and in next dc, ch 1, skip next dc, dc in next dc) 4 times, ★ 2 dc in next ch-5 sp, ch 5, skip next sc, sc in next 3 sc, ch 5, 2 dc in next ch-5 sp, dc in next dc, ch 1, skip next dc, dc in next dc; repeat from ★ 4 times **more**, (dc in next ch-1 sp and in next dc, ch 1, skip next dc, dc in next dc) across: 56 dc, 15 sc, and 24 sps.

Row 23: Ch 3, turn; (dc in next ch-1 sp and in next dc, ch 1, skip next dc, dc in next dc) 5 times, 2 dc in next ch-5 sp, ch 5, skip next sc, sc in next sc, ch 5, 2 dc in next ch-5 sp, dc in next dc, ★ ch 1, skip next dc, dc in next dc, dc in next ch-1 sp and in next dc, ch 1, skip next dc, dc in next dc, 2 dc in next ch-5 sp, ch 5, skip next sc, sc in next sc, ch 5, 2 dc in next ch-5 sp, dc in next dc; repeat from ★ 3 times **more**, (ch 1, skip next dc, dc in next dc, dc in next ch-1 sp and in next dc) across: 72 dc, 5 sc, and 28 sps.

Row 24: Ch 4, turn; skip next dc, dc in next dc, (dc in next ch-1 sp and in next dc, ch 1, skip next dc, dc in next dc) 5 times, 2 dc in next ch-5 sp, ch 1, 2 dc in next ch-5 sp, dc in next dc, ch 1, skip next dc, dc in next dc, ★ (dc in next ch-1 sp and in next dc, ch 1, skip next dc, dc in next dc) twice, 2 dc in next ch-5 sp, ch 1, 2 dc in next ch-5 sp, dc in next dc, ch 1, skip next dc, dc in next dc; repeat from ★ 3 times **more**, (dc in next ch-1 sp and in next dc, ch 1, skip next dc, dc in next dc) across: 86 dc and 29 ch-1 sps.

Row 25: Ch 3, turn; dc in next ch-1 sp and in next dc, ★ ch 1, skip next dc, dc in next dc, dc in next ch-1 sp and in next dc; repeat from ★ across: 87 dc and 28 ch-1 sps.

Rows 26-57: Repeat Rows 18-25, 4 times.

Row 58: Ch 4, turn; skip next dc, dc in next dc, ★ dc in next ch-1 sp and in next dc, ch 1, skip next dc, dc in next dc; repeat from ★ across: 86 dc and 29 ch-1 sps.

Row 59: Ch 3, turn; dc in next ch-1 sp and in next dc, ★ ch 1, skip next dc, dc in next dc, dc in next ch-1 sp and in next dc; repeat from ★ across: 87 dc and 28 ch-1 sps.

Rows 60-73: Repeat Rows 58 and 59, 7 times; at end of Row 73, do **not** finish off.

EDGING

Rnd 1: Ch 5, do **not** turn; dc in last dc made on Row 73; work 161 dc evenly spaced across end of rows; working in free loops of beginning ch *(Fig. 2b, page 91)*, (dc, ch 2, dc) in first ch, dc in each ch and in each sp across to marked ch, (dc, ch 2, dc) in marked ch; work 161 dc evenly spaced across end of rows; (dc, ch 2, dc) in first dc on Row 73, dc in each dc and in each ch-1 sp across; join with slip st to first dc: 556 dc and 4 ch-2 sps.

Rnd 2: Slip st in next ch-2 sp, ch 6 **(counts as first dc plus ch 3, now and throughout)**, dc in same sp, ch 1, dc in next dc, ch 1, ★ (skip next dc, dc in next dc, ch 1) across to next corner ch-2 sp, (dc, ch 3, dc) in corner ch-2 sp, ch 1, dc in next dc, ch 1; repeat from ★ 2 times **more**, (skip next dc, dc in next dc, ch 1) across; join with slip st to first dc: 288 dc and 288 sps.

Rnd 3: (Slip st, ch 3, dc, ch 2, 2 dc) in next ch-3 sp, ★ dc in each dc and in each ch-1 sp across to next corner ch-3 sp, (2 dc, ch 2, 2 dc) in corner ch-3 sp; repeat from ★ 2 times **more**, dc in each dc and in each ch-1 sp across; join with slip st to first dc: 588 dc and 4 ch-2 sps.

Rnd 4: Slip st in next dc and in next ch-2 sp, ch 6, dc in same sp, ch 1, dc in next dc, ch 1, ★ (skip next dc, dc in next dc, ch 1) across to next corner ch-2 sp, (dc, ch 3, dc) in corner ch-2 sp, ch 1, dc in next dc, ch 1; repeat from ★ 2 times **more**, (skip next dc, dc in next dc, ch 1) across; join with slip st to first dc: 304 dc and 304 sps.

Rnd 5: (Slip st, ch 3, dc, ch 3, 2 dc) in next ch-3 sp, ★ ♥ dc in next dc, ch 5, skip next 2 ch-1 sps and next dc, sc in next ch-1 sp, (sc in next dc and in next ch-1 sp) twice, ch 5, skip next 2 dc and next ch-1 sp, dc in next dc, † dc in next ch-1 sp and in next dc, ch 5, skip next 2 ch-1 sps and next dc, sc in next ch-1 sp, (sc in next dc and in next ch-1 sp) twice, ch 5, skip next 2 dc and next ch-1 sp, dc in next dc †; repeat from † to † across to next corner ch-3 sp ♥, (2 dc, ch 3, 2 dc) in corner ch-3 sp; repeat from ★ 2 times **more**, then repeat from ♥ to ♥ once; join with slip st to first dc: 80 sps.

Rnd 6: Slip st in next dc and in next ch-3 sp, ch 3, (dc, ch 3, 2 dc) in same sp, dc in next dc, ch 1, skip next dc, dc in next dc, ★ † 2 dc in next ch-5 sp, ch 5, skip next sc, sc in next 3 sc, ch 5, 2 dc in next ch-5 sp, dc in next dc, ch 1, skip next st, dc in next st †; repeat from † to † across to next corner ch-3 sp, (2 dc, ch 3, 2 dc) in corner ch-3 sp, dc in next dc, ch 1, skip next dc, dc in next dc; repeat from ★ 2 times **more**, then repeat from † to † across; join with slip st to first dc: 122 sps.

Rnd 7: Slip st in next dc and in next ch-3 sp, ch 3, (dc, ch 3, 2 dc) in same sp, ★ ♥ dc in next dc, ch 5, sc in next ch-1 sp, ch 5, skip next 2 dc, dc in next dc, † 2 dc in next ch-5 sp, ch 5, skip next sc, sc in next sc, ch 5, 2 dc in next ch-5 sp, dc in next dc, ch 5, sc in next ch-1 sp, ch 5, skip next 2 sts, dc in next st †; repeat from † to † across to next corner ch-3 sp ♥, (2 dc, ch 3, 2 dc) in corner ch-3 sp; repeat from ★ 2 times **more**, then repeat from ♥ to ♥ once; join with slip st to first dc: 164 sps.

Rnd 8: Slip st in next dc and in next ch-3 sp, ch 3, (dc, ch 3, 2 dc) in same sp, ★ ♥ dc in next dc, ch 3, sc in next ch-5 sp, ch 5, sc in next ch-5 sp, ch 3, skip next 2 dc, dc in next dc, † 2 dc in next ch-5 sp, ch 1, 2 dc in next ch-5 sp, dc in next dc, ch 3, sc in next ch-5 sp, ch 5, sc in next ch-5 sp, ch 3, skip next 2 sts, dc in next st †; repeat from † to † across to next corner ch-3 sp ♥, (2 dc, ch 3, 2 dc) in corner ch-3 sp; repeat from ★ 2 times **more**, then repeat from ♥ to ♥ once; join with slip st to first dc: 168 sps.

Rnd 9: Slip st in next dc and in next ch-3 sp, ch 3, (dc, ch 3, 2 dc) in same sp, ★ ♥ dc in next dc, ch 3, sc in next ch-3 sp, work Cluster in next ch-5 sp, (ch 2, work Cluster in same sp) 4 times, sc in next ch-3 sp, ch 3, skip next 2 dc, dc in next dc, † dc in next ch-1 sp and in next dc, ch 3, sc in next ch-3 sp, work Cluster in next ch-5 sp, (ch 2, work Cluster in same sp) 4 times, sc in next ch-3 sp, ch 3, skip next 2 sts, dc in next st †; repeat from † to † across to next corner ch-3 sp ♥, (2 dc, ch 3, 2 dc) in corner ch-3 sp; repeat from ★ 2 times **more**, then repeat from ♥ to ♥ once; join with slip st to first dc.

Rnd 10: Slip st in next dc and in next ch-3 sp, ch 1, (3 sc, work Picot, 2 sc) in same sp, ★ ♥ sc in next 3 dc, † (2 sc, work Picot, sc) in next ch-3 sp, sc in next sc, (sc, work Picot, sc) in next ch-2 sp, [sc in next Cluster, (sc, work Picot, sc) in next ch-2 sp] 3 times, skip next Cluster, sc in next sc, (2 sc, work Picot, sc) in next ch-3 sp, sc in next 3 sts †; repeat from † to † across to next corner ch-3 sp ♥, (3 sc, work Picot, 2 sc) in corner ch-3 sp; repeat from ★ 2 times **more**, then repeat from ♥ to ♥ once; join with slip st to first sc, finish off.

Design by Kay Meadors. ●

little boy blue

■■■□ **INTERMEDIATE**

Finished Size: 35" x 48½" (89 cm x 123 cm)

MATERIALS

Light Weight Yarn **[3 LIGHT]**
[5 ounces, 468 yards
(140 grams, 429 meters) per skein]:
4 skeins
Crochet hook, size F (3.75 mm) **or** size needed
for gauge

GAUGE: In pattern, 16 dc and 8 rows = 4" (10 cm)

Gauge Swatch: 4¼"w x 4"h (10.75 cm x 10 cm)
Ch 19.
Work same as Afghan Body Rows 1-8.
Finish off.

STITCH GUIDE

FRONT POST DOUBLE CROCHET
(abbreviated FPdc)
YO, insert hook from **front** to **back** around post of
st indicated **(Fig. 6, page 93)**, YO and pull up a loop
(3 loops on hook), (YO and draw through 2 loops on
hook) twice. Skip st behind FPdc.

BACK POST DOUBLE CROCHET
(abbreviated BPdc)
YO, insert hook from **back** to **front** around post
of FPdc indicated **(Fig. 6, page 93)**, YO and pull
up a loop (3 loops on hook), (YO and draw through
2 loops on hook) twice. Skip st in front of BPdc.

FRONT POST CLUSTER
(abbreviated FP Cluster)
★ YO, insert hook from **front** to **back** around post
of st indicated **(Fig. 6, page 93)**, YO and pull up a
loop, YO and draw through 2 loops on hook; repeat
from ★ once **more**, YO and draw through all 3 loops
on hook. Skip st behind FP Cluster.

AFGHAN BODY

Ch 127; place a marker in third ch from hook for st
placement.

Row 1: Dc in fourth ch from hook **(3 skipped chs
count as first dc)** and in each ch across: 125 dc.

Row 2 (Right side)**:** Ch 3 **(counts as first dc, now
and throughout)**, turn; dc in next 4 dc, ★ work FPdc
around next dc, dc in next 2 dc, work FP Cluster around
next dc, dc in next 2 dc, work FPdc around next dc, dc
in next 5 dc; repeat from ★ across: 95 dc, 20 FPdc, and
10 FP Clusters.

Note: Loop a short piece of yarn around any stitch to
mark Row 2 as **right** side.

Row 3: Ch 3, turn; dc in next 4 dc, (work BPdc around
next FPdc, dc in next 5 sts) across: 105 dc and 20 BPdc.

Row 4: Ch 3, turn; dc in next dc, work FP Cluster
around next dc, dc in next 2 dc, ★ work FPdc around
next BPdc, dc in next 5 dc, work FPdc around next BPdc,
dc in next 2 dc, work FP Cluster around next dc, dc in
next 2 dc; repeat from ★ across: 94 dc, 20 FPdc, and
11 FP Clusters.

Row 5: Ch 3, turn; dc in next 4 sts, (work BPdc around
next FPdc, dc in next 5 sts) across: 105 dc and 20 BPdc.

Row 6: Ch 3, turn; dc in next 4 dc, ★ work FPdc around
next BPdc, dc in next 2 dc, work FP Cluster around next
dc, dc in next 2 dc, work FPdc around next BPdc, dc in
next 5 dc; repeat from ★ across: 95 dc, 20 FPdc, and
10 FP Clusters.

Repeat Rows 3-6 for pattern until Afghan Body measures
approximately 44½" (113 cm) from beginning ch, ending
by working a **wrong** side row; do **not** finish off.

EDGING

Rnd 1 (Right side)**:** Ch 3, turn; (2 dc, ch 1, 3 dc) in first dc, dc in each st across to last dc, (3 dc, ch 1, 3 dc) in last dc; work 177 dc evenly spaced across end of rows; working in free loops of beginning ch *(Fig. 2b, page 91)*, (3 dc, ch 1, 3 dc) in marked ch, dc in each ch across to last ch, (3 dc, ch 1, 3 dc) in last ch; work 177 dc evenly spaced across end of rows; join with slip st to first dc: 624 dc and 4 ch-1 sps.

Rnd 2: Ch 3, do **not** turn; skip next dc, work FP Cluster around next dc, ch 3, skip next corner ch-1 sp, work FP Cluster around next dc, ★ skip next dc, dc in next 5 dc, (work FP Cluster around next dc, dc in next 5 dc) across to within 2 dc of next corner ch-1 sp, skip next dc, work FP Cluster around next dc, ch 3, skip next corner ch-1 sp, work FP Cluster around next dc; repeat from ★ 2 times **more**, skip next dc, (dc in next 5 dc, work FP Cluster around next dc) across to last 4 dc, dc in last 4 dc; join with slip st to first dc: 510 dc, 106 FP Clusters, and 4 ch-3 sps.

Rnd 3: Slip st in next FP Cluster and in next corner ch-3 sp, ch 3, (2 dc, ch 1, 3 dc) in same sp, work FP Cluster around next FP Cluster, skip next dc, dc in next 3 dc, ★ † skip next dc, work (FP Cluster, ch 3, FP Cluster) around next FP Cluster, skip next dc, dc in next 3 dc †; repeat from † to † across to within 2 sts of next corner ch-3 sp, skip next dc, work FP Cluster around next FP Cluster, (3 dc, ch 1, 3 dc) in next corner ch-3 sp, work FP Cluster around next FP Cluster, skip next dc, dc in next 3 dc; repeat from ★ 2 times **more**, then repeat from † to † across to last 2 sts, skip next st, work FP Cluster around last FP Cluster; join with slip st to first dc: 330 dc, 204 FP Clusters, and 102 sps.

Rnd 4: Ch 1, **turn**; sc in same st as joining and in each st around, working 3 sc in each ch-3 sp and one sc in each ch-1 sp; join with slip st to first sc, finish off.

Design by Mary Ann Sipes. ●

pineapple parade

INTERMEDIATE

Finished Size: 36" x 46" (91.5 cm x 117 cm)

MATERIALS
Light Weight Yarn **3 LIGHT**
[5.6 ounces, 431 yards
(160 grams, 394 meters) per skein]:
   Pink - 4 skeins
   Variegated - 2 skeins
Crochet hook, size F (3.75 mm) **or** size needed
   for gauge
Yarn needle

GAUGE: Rows 3-14 = 5½" (14 cm)
Each Strip = 5¼" (13.25 cm) at widest point

Gauge Swatch: 4¼"w x 3¾"h (10.75 cm x 9.5 cm)
Work same as Strip A through Row 7.

STITCH GUIDE
BEGINNING SHELL
Turn; skip first dc, slip st in next dc and in next
ch-2 sp, ch 3, (dc, ch 2, 2 dc) in same sp.
SHELL
(2 Dc, ch 2, 2 dc) in sp indicated.
SCALLOP
(Slip st, ch 2, hdc) in st indicated.
DECREASE (uses next 2 dc)
YO, insert hook in same st as joining on same strip,
YO and pull up a loop, YO and draw through 2 loops
on hook, YO, skip next joining, insert hook in same
st as joining on next strip, YO and pull up a loop, YO
and draw through 2 loops on hook, YO and draw
through all 3 loops on hook.

STRIP A (Make 5)
With Pink, ch 4; join with slip st to form a ring.

Row 1: Ch 3 **(counts as first dc, now and throughout)**, dc in ring, (ch 2, 2 dc in ring) twice: 6 dc and 2 ch-2 sps.

Row 2 (Right side)**:** Work Beginning Shell, ch 1, work Shell in last ch-2 sp: 8 dc and 3 sps.

Note: Loop a short piece of yarn around any stitch to mark Row 2 as **right** side and bottom edge.

Row 3: Work Beginning Shell, ch 1, dc in next ch-1 sp, ch 1, work Shell in last ch-2 sp: 9 dc and 4 sps.

Row 4: Work Beginning Shell, ch 1, skip next ch-1 sp, (dc, ch 3, dc) in next dc, ch 1, skip next ch-1 sp, work Shell in last ch-2 sp: 10 dc and 5 sps.

Row 5: Work Beginning Shell, ch 1, skip next ch-1 sp, 7 dc in next ch-3 sp, ch 1, skip next ch-1 sp, work Shell in last ch-2 sp: 15 dc and 4 sps.

Row 6: Work Beginning Shell, ch 1, skip next ch-1 sp, (hdc in next dc, ch 1) 7 times, skip next ch-1 sp, work Shell in last ch-2 sp: 10 sps.

Row 7: Work Beginning Shell, ch 2, skip next ch-1 sp, (sc in next ch-1 sp, ch 2) 6 times, skip next ch-1 sp, work Shell in last ch-2 sp: 9 ch-2 sps.

Row 8: Work Beginning Shell, ch 2, skip next ch-2 sp, (sc in next ch-2 sp, ch 2) 5 times, skip next ch-2 sp, work Shell in last ch-2 sp: 8 ch-2 sps.

Row 9: Work Beginning Shell, ch 2, skip next ch-2 sp, (sc in next ch-2 sp, ch 2) 4 times, skip next ch-2 sp, work Shell in last ch-2 sp: 7 ch-2 sps.

Row 10: Work Beginning Shell, ch 2, skip next ch-2 sp, (sc in next ch-2 sp, ch 2) 3 times, skip next ch-2 sp, work Shell in last ch-2 sp: 6 ch-2 sps.

Row 11: Work Beginning Shell, ch 2, skip next ch-2 sp, (sc in next ch-2 sp, ch 2) twice, skip next ch-2 sp, work Shell in last ch-2 sp: 5 ch-2 sps.

Row 12: Work Beginning Shell, ch 2, skip next ch-2 sp, sc in next ch-2 sp, ch 2, skip next ch-2 sp, work Shell in last ch-2 sp: 4 ch-2 sps.

Row 13: Work Beginning Shell, skip next 2 ch-2 sps, work Shell in last ch-2 sp: 8 dc and 2 ch-2 sps.

Row 14: Work Beginning Shell, ch 1, work Shell in last ch-2 sp: 3 sps.

Rows 15-96: Repeat Rows 3-14, 6 times; then repeat Rows 3-12 once **more**: 4 ch-2 sps.

Instructions continued on page 45.

shining star

Finished Size: 31½" x 40" (80 cm x 101.5 cm)

MATERIALS

Medium Weight Yarn **4** MEDIUM

[3.5 ounces, 200 yards
(100 grams, 182 meters) per skein]:
6 skeins
Crochet hook, size J (6 mm) **or** size needed
for gauge

GAUGE: In pattern, (sc, ch 3) 4 times
and 8 rows = 3½" (9 cm)

Gauge Swatch: 7¼"w x 4¼"h (18.5 cm x 10.75 cm)
Ch 26.
Work same as Afghan Body Rows 1-9.
Finish off.

STITCH GUIDE

PICOT
Ch 3, slip st in third ch from hook.

AFGHAN BODY

Ch 86.

Row 1: Sc in second ch from hook, ★ ch 3, skip next
2 chs, sc in next ch; repeat from ★ across: 29 sc and
28 ch-3 sps.

Row 2 (Right side)**:** Ch 3 **(counts as first dc, now and
throughout)**, turn; dc in same st, sc in next ch-3 sp,
(ch 3, sc in next ch-3 sp) 3 times, ★ 3 dc in next sc, sc
in next ch-3 sp, (ch 3, sc in next ch-3 sp) 3 times; repeat
from ★ across to last sc, 2 dc in last sc: 22 dc and
21 ch-3 sps.

Row 3: Ch 3, turn; dc in same st, 2 dc in next dc, sc in
next ch-3 sp, (ch 3, sc in next ch-3 sp) twice, ★ skip next
sc, 2 dc in each of next 3 dc, sc in next ch-3 sp, (ch 3,
sc in next ch-3 sp) twice; repeat from ★ across to last
3 sts, skip next sc, 2 dc in each of last 2 dc: 44 dc and
14 ch-3 sps: 44 dc and 14 ch-3 sps.

Row 4: Ch 3, turn; 2 dc in each of next 2 dc, dc in next
dc, sc in next ch-3 sp, ch 3, sc in next ch-3 sp, skip next
sc, dc in next dc, ★ 2 dc in each of next 4 dc, dc in next
dc, sc in next ch-3 sp, ch 3, sc in next ch-3 sp, skip next
sc, dc in next dc; repeat from ★ across to last 3 sts, 2 dc
in each of next 2 dc, dc in last dc: 72 dc and 7 ch-3 sps.

Row 5: Ch 1, turn; sc in first dc, ch 3, skip next 3 dc,
in sp **before** next dc **(Fig. 8, page 93)**, ch 3, sc in next
ch-3 sp, ch 3, ★ (skip next 3 sts, sc in sp **before** next
dc, ch 3) 3 times, sc in next ch-3 sp, ch 3; repeat from
★ across to last 7 sts, skip next 3 sts, sc in sp **before**
next dc, ch 3, skip next 3 dc, sc in last dc: 29 sc and
28 ch-3 sps.

Row 6: Ch 5 **(counts as first dc plus ch 2, now and
throughout)**, turn; sc in next ch-3 sp, ch 3, sc in next
ch-3 sp, 3 dc in next sc, sc in next ch-3 sp, ★ (ch 3, sc in
next ch-3 sp) 3 times, 3 dc in next sc, sc in next ch-3 sp;
repeat from ★ across to last ch-3 sp, ch 3, sc in last
ch-3 sp, ch 2, dc in last sc: 23 dc and 22 sps.

Row 7: Ch 1, turn; sc in first dc, ch 3, skip next ch-2 sp,
sc in next ch-3 sp, skip next sc, 2 dc in each of next 3 dc,
sc in next ch-3 sp, ★ (ch 3, sc in next ch-3 sp) twice, skip
next sc, 2 dc in each of next 3 dc, sc in next ch-3 sp;
repeat from ★ across to last ch-2 sp, ch 3, skip last
ch-2 sp, sc in last dc: 42 dc and 14 ch-3 sps.

Row 8: Ch 5, turn; sc in next ch-3 sp, ★ † skip next sc,
dc in next dc, 2 dc in each of next 4 dc, dc in next dc, sc
in next ch-3 sp †, ch 3, sc in next ch-3 sp; repeat from ★
5 times **more**, then repeat from † to † once, ch 2, dc in
last sc: 72 dc and 8 sps.

Instructions continued on page 44.

Row 9: Ch 1, turn; sc in first dc, ch 3, skip next sc and next 2 dc, sc in sp **before** next dc, ch 3, (skip next 3 dc, sc in sp **before** next dc, ch 3) twice, ★ sc in next ch-3 sp, ch 3, (skip next 3 sts, sc in sp **before** next dc, ch 3) 3 times; repeat from ★ across to last ch-2 sp, skip last ch-2 sp, sc in last dc: 29 sc and 28 ch-3 sps.

Rows 10-77: Repeat Rows 2-9, 8 times; then repeat Rows 2-5 once **more**; at end of last row, do **not** finish off.

EDGING

Rnd 1: Ch 1, turn; 2 sc in first sc, work 93 sc evenly spaced across to last sc, 3 sc in last sc; work 129 sc evenly spaced across end of rows; working in free loops of beginning ch **(Fig. 2b, page 91)**, 3 sc in ch at base of first sc, work 93 sc evenly spaced across to last ch, 3 sc in last ch; work 129 sc evenly spaced across end of rows, sc in same st as first sc; join with slip st to first sc: 456 sc.

Rnd 2: Ch 1, do **not** turn; sc in same st, ch 3, ★ skip next 2 sc, (sc in next sc, ch 3, skip next 2 sc) across to center sc of next corner 3-sc group, (sc, ch 3) twice in center sc; repeat from ★ 2 times **more**, skip next sc, (sc in next sc, ch 3, skip next 2 sc) across, sc in same st as first sc, ch 1, hdc in first sc to form last corner ch-3 sp; 156 sc and 156 ch-3 sps.

Rnds 3-6: Ch 1, sc in last ch-3 sp made, ch 3, ★ (sc in next ch-3 sp, ch 3) across to next corner ch-3 sp, (sc, ch 3) twice in corner ch-3 sp; repeat from ★ 2 times **more**, (sc in next ch-3 sp, ch 3) across, sc in same sp as first sc, ch 1, hdc in first sc to form last corner ch-3 sp: 172 sc and 172 ch-3 sps.

Rnd 7: Ch 1, sc in last ch-3 sp made, ★ † 3 dc in next sc, [sc in next ch-3 sp, (ch 3, sc in next ch-3 sp) 3 times, 3 dc in next sc] across to next corner ch-3 sp †, (sc, ch 3 sc) in corner ch-3 sp; repeat from ★ 2 times **more**, then repeat from † to † once, sc in same sp as first sc, ch 1, hdc in first sc to form last corner ch-3 sp: 138 dc and 130 ch-3 sps.

Rnd 8: Ch 1, sc in last ch-3 sp made, ★ † skip next sc, 2 dc in each of next 3 dc, [sc in next ch-3 sp, (ch 3, sc in next ch-3 sp) twice, skip next sc, 2 dc in each of next 3 dc] across to next corner ch-3 sp †, (sc, ch 3, sc) in corner ch-3 sp; repeat from ★ 2 times **more**, then repeat from † to † once, sc in same sp as first sc, ch 1, hdc in first sc to form last corner ch-3 sp: 276 dc and 88 ch-3 sps.

Rnd 9: Ch 1, sc in last ch-3 sp made, ★ † skip next sc, dc in next dc, 2 dc in each of next 4 dc, dc in next dc, [sc in next ch-3 sp, ch 3, sc in next ch-3 sp, skip next sc, dc in next dc, 2 dc in each of next 4 dc, dc in next dc] across to next corner ch-3 sp †, (sc, ch 3, sc) in corner ch-3 sp; repeat from ★ 2 times **more**, then repeat from † to † once, sc in same sp as first sc, ch 1, hdc in first sc to form last corner ch-3 sp: 460 and 46 ch-3 sps.

Rnd 10: Ch 1, (sc, ch 3) twice in last ch-3 sp made, skip next 3 sts, sc in sp **before** next dc, ch 3, (skip next 2 dc, sc in sp **before** next dc, ch 3) 3 times, ★ (sc, ch 3) twice in next ch-3 sp, skip next 3 sts, sc in sp **before** next dc, ch 3, (skip next 2 dc, sc in sp **before** next dc, ch 3) 3 times; repeat from ★ around; join with slip st to first sc, finish off.

Design by Kay Meadors. ●

Row 97: Turn; skip first dc, slip st in next dc and in next ch-2 sp, ch 3, (dc, ch 1, 2 dc) in same sp, skip next 2 ch-2 sps, (2 dc, ch 1, 2 dc) in last ch-2 sp: 2 ch-1 sps.

Row 98: Turn; skip first dc, slip st in next dc and in next ch-1 sp, ch 3, YO, insert hook in same sp, YO and pull up a loop, YO and draw through 2 loops on hook, YO, insert hook in next ch-1 sp, YO and pull up a loop, YO and draw through 2 loops on hook, YO and draw through all 3 loops on hook, dc in same sp; finish off: 3 sts.

BORDER

With **right** side facing, join Variegated with dc in beginning ring **(see Joining With Dc, page 91)**; (ch 1, dc) twice in same sp; working around dc at end of rows, (dc, ch 1, dc) in first row, 2 dc in each of next 4 rows, ♥ (dc, ch 1, dc) in next 2 rows, place marker around last dc made for joining and st placement, ch 1, dc in same row, ★ † (dc, ch 1, dc) in next row, 2 dc in each of next 3 rows, dc in next 3 rows, 2 dc in each of next 3 rows †, (dc, ch 1, dc) in next row, dc in next row, (ch 1, dc in same row) twice; repeat from ★ 5 times **more**, then repeat from † to † once, (dc, ch 1, dc) in each of next 2 rows, place marker around last dc made for joining and st placement, ch 1, dc in same row, (dc, ch 1, dc) in next row ♥, 2 dc in each of next 5 rows, (dc, ch 1, dc) in last row, skip first dc on Row 98, dc in next st, (ch 1, dc in same st) twice; working around dc at end of rows, (dc, ch 1, dc) in same row, 2 dc in each of next 5 rows, repeat from ♥ to ♥ once, 2 dc in each of next 4 rows, (dc, ch 1, dc) in last row; join with slip st to first dc, finish off.

STRIP B (Make 4)

Work same as Strip A through Row 84: 4 ch-2 sps.

Rows 85 and 86: Work same as Rows 97 and 98 of Strip A.

BORDER

With **right** side facing, join Variegated with dc in beginning ring; (ch 1, dc) twice in same sp; working around dc at end of rows, (dc, ch 1, dc) in first row, † dc in next row, place marker around dc just made for joining and st placement, dc in same row, 2 dc in each of next 3 rows, (dc, ch 1, dc) in next row, dc in next row, ch 1, dc in same row) twice, (dc, ch 1, dc) in next row,

★ 2 dc in each of next 3 rows, dc in next 3 rows, 2 dc in each of next 3 rows, (dc, ch 1, dc) in next row, dc in next row, (ch 1, dc in same row) twice, (dc, ch 1, dc) in next row; repeat from ★ 5 times **more**, 2 dc in each of next 4 rows, place marker around last dc made for joining and st placement †, 2 dc in next row, (dc, ch 1, dc) in last row, skip first dc on Row 86, dc in next st, (ch 1, dc in same st) twice; working around dc at end of rows, (dc, ch 1, dc) in same row, 2 dc in next row, repeat from † to † once, (dc, ch 1, dc) in last row; join with slip st to first dc, finish off.

ASSEMBLY

Afghan is assembled by joining Strips in the following order: Strip A, (Strip B, Strip A) 4 times.

Join Strips as follows:
With Variegated, having bottom edges at same end and working through **both** loops of each st on **both** pieces, whipstitch Strips together **(Fig. 10a, page 94)**, beginning in first marked dc and ending in next marked dc.

EDGING

Remove 2 markers from unjoined edge of each outer Strip A (4 markers total). When working Edging, dc and chs count as sts.

With **right** side of top edge facing, join Variegated with slip st in ch before center dc at top point on first Strip A; ch 2, hdc in same st, ★ † (skip next st, work Scallop in next st) across to within 3 sts of next joined dc, skip next dc, slip st in next dc, skip next st, decrease; repeat from ★ 7 times **more**, skip next ch †, (work Scallop in next st, skip next st) 26 times, slip st in next 2 dc, [(work Scallop in next st, skip next st) 12 times, slip st in next 2 dc] 6 times, work Scallop in next dc, repeat from † to † once, (work Scallop in next st, skip next st) 24 times, slip st in next 2 dc, [(work Scallop in next st, skip next st) 12 times, slip st in next 2 dc] 6 times, (work Scallop in next st, skip next st) across; join with slip st to first slip st, finish off.

Design by Anne Halliday. ●

pineapple patch

Finished Size: 36" x 50" (91.5 cm x 127 cm)

MATERIALS

Light Weight Yarn 🧶 **3**
[5.6 ounces, 431 yards
(160 grams, 394 meters) per skein]:
   Variegated - 3 skeins
   Yellow - 2 skeins
Crochet hook, size F (3.75 mm) **or** size needed
   for gauge
Yarn needle

GAUGE: Each Motif = 7" (17.75 cm)
   (straight edge to straight edge)
   Each Square = 3" (7.5 cm)

Gauge Swatch: 4½"w x 5¼"h (11.5 cm x 13.25 cm)
Work same as Motif Center.

STITCH GUIDE

TREBLE CROCHET (abbreviated tr)
YO twice, insert hook in st indicated, YO and pull
up a loop (4 loops on hook), (YO and draw through
2 loops on hook) 3 times.
BEGINNING SHELL
Turn; skip first dc, slip st in next dc and in next
ch-2 sp, ch 3, (dc, ch 2, 2 dc) in same sp.
SHELL
(2 Dc, ch 2, 2 dc) in sp indicated.
CLUSTER (uses next 3 dc)
★ YO, insert hook in **next** dc, YO and pull up a loop,
YO and draw through 2 loops on hook; repeat from
★ 2 times **more**, YO and draw through all 4 loops
on hook.

MOTIF (Make 35)
CENTER

With Yellow, ch 7; join with slip st to form a ring.

Row 1 (Right side)**:** Ch 3 **(counts as first dc, now
and throughout)**, dc in ring, (ch 2, 2 dc in ring) 3 times:
3 ch-2 sps.

Note: Loop a short piece of yarn around any stitch to
mark Row 1 as **right** side and bottom edge.

Row 2: Work Beginning Shell, ch 2, (dc, ch 3, dc) in next
ch-2 sp, ch 2, work Shell in last ch-2 sp: 5 sps.

Row 3: Work Beginning Shell, ch 3, skip next ch-2 sp,
8 dc in next ch-3 sp, ch 3, skip next ch-2 sp, work Shell in
last ch-2 sp: 16 dc and 4 sps.

Row 4: Work Beginning Shell, ch 3, skip next ch-3 sp, sc
in next sc, (ch 1, sc in next dc) 7 times, ch 3, skip next
ch-3 sp, work Shell in last ch-2 sp: 11 sps.

Row 5: Work Beginning Shell, ch 3, skip next ch-3 sp, sc
in next ch-1 sp, (ch 1, sc in next ch-1 sp) 6 times, ch 3,
skip next ch-3 sp, work Shell in last ch-2 sp: 10 sps.

Row 6: Work Beginning Shell, ch 3, skip next ch-3 sp, sc
in next ch-1 sp, (ch 1, sc in next ch-1 sp) 5 times, ch 3,
skip next ch-3 sp, work Shell in last ch-2 sp: 9 sps.

Row 7: Work Beginning Shell, ch 3, skip next ch-3 sp, sc
in next ch-1 sp, (ch 1, sc in next ch-1 sp) 4 times, ch 3,
skip next ch-3 sp, work Shell in last ch-2 sp: 8 sps.

Row 8: Work Beginning Shell, ch 3, skip next ch-3 sp, sc
in next ch-1 sp, (ch 1, sc in next ch-1 sp) 3 times, ch 3,
skip next ch-3 sp, work Shell in last ch-2 sp: 7 sps.

Row 9: Work Beginning Shell, ch 3, skip next ch-3 sp, sc
in next ch-1 sp, (ch 1, sc in next ch-1 sp) twice, ch 3, skip
next ch-3 sp, work Shell in last ch-2 sp: 6 sps.

Instructions continued on page 48

Row 10: Work Beginning Shell, ch 3, skip next ch-3 sp, sc in next ch-1 sp, ch 1, sc in next ch-1 sp, ch 3, skip next ch-3 sp, work Shell in last ch-2 sp: 5 sps.

Row 11: Turn; skip first dc, slip st in next dc and in next ch-2 sp, ch 3, (dc, ch 3, 2 dc) in same sp, ch 2, skip next ch-3 sp, sc in next ch-1 sp, ch 2, skip next ch-3 sp, 2 dc in last ch-2 sp, ch 1, drop loop from hook, insert hook from **front** to **back** in center ch of last ch-3 made, hook dropped loop and draw through, ch 1, 2 dc in same sp as last dc made; ch 3, **turn**; skip next 2 sps and next dc; join with slip st in last dc, finish off: one ch-3 sp.

BORDER

Rnd 1: With **right** side facing, join Variegated with sc in beginning ring *(see Joining With Sc, page 91)*; ch 3, (sc around dc at end of next row, ch 3) 11 times, sc in next ch-3 sp on Row 11; (ch 3, sc around dc at end of next row) 11 times, ch 1, dc in first sc to form last ch-3 sp: 24 ch-3 sps.

Rnd 2: (Ch 4, sc in next ch-3 sp) around, ch 2, dc in joining dc to form last ch-4 sp.

Rnd 3: (Ch 4, sc in next ch-4 sp) twice, ch 5, ★ sc in next ch-4 sp, (ch 4, sc in next ch-4 sp) twice, ch 5; repeat from ★ around; join with slip st to joining dc.

Rnd 4: Slip st in first ch and in ch-4 sp, ch 3, 2 dc in same sp, ch 1, 3 dc in next ch-4 sp, ch 1, (dc, ch 3, dc) in next ch-5 sp, ch 1, ★ (3 dc in next ch-4 sp, ch 1) twice, (dc, ch 3, dc) in next ch-5 sp, ch 1; repeat from ★ around; join with slip st to first dc, finish off: 64 dc, 24 ch-1 sps, and 8 ch-3 sps.

SQUARE (Make 24)

Rnd 1 (Right side)**:** With Yellow, ch 4, 2 dc in fourth ch from hook **(3 skipped chs count as first dc)**, (ch 3, 3 dc in same ch) 3 times, ch 1, dc in first dc to form last ch-3 sp: 12 dc and 4 ch-3 sps.

Note: Mark Rnd 1 as **right** side.

Rnd 2: Ch 6, dc in last ch-3 sp made, ch 2, work Cluster, ch 2, ★ (dc, ch 3, dc) in next ch-3 sp, ch 2, work Cluster, ch 2; repeat from ★ 2 times **more**; join with slip st to third ch of beginning ch-6, finish off: 12 sts and 12 sps.

Rnd 3: With **right** side facing, join Variegated with dc in any corner ch-3 sp *(see Joining With Dc, page 91)*; ch 3, dc in same sp, ch 1, dc in next dc, 2 dc in next ch-2 sp, ch 1, 2 dc in next ch-2 sp, dc in next dc, ch 1, ★ (dc, ch 3, dc) in next corner ch-3 sp, ch 1, dc in next dc, 2 dc in next ch-2 sp, ch 1, 2 dc in next ch-2 sp, dc in next dc, ch 1; repeat from ★ 2 times **more**; join with slip st to first dc, finish off: 32 dc and 16 sps.

TRIANGLE (Make 20)

Row 1 (Right side)**:** With Variegated, ch 6, place marker in second ch from hook for st placement, (3 dc, ch 3, 3 dc, ch 1, tr) in sixth ch from hook: 7 sts and 3 sps.

Note: Mark Row 1 as **right** side.

Row 2: Ch 5 **(counts as first tr plus ch 1, now and throughout)**, turn; dc in next ch-1 sp, ch 2, work Cluster, ch 2, (dc, ch 3, dc) in next ch-3 sp, ch 2, work Cluster, ch 2, dc in next sp, ch 1, tr in marked ch: 8 sts and 7 sps.

Row 3: Ch 5, turn; dc in next ch-1 sp, ch 1, dc in next dc, 2 dc in next ch-2 sp, ch 1, 2 dc in next ch-2 sp, dc in next dc, ch 1, (dc, ch 3, dc) in next ch-3 sp, ch 1, dc in next dc, 2 dc in next ch-2 sp, ch 1, 2 dc in next ch-2 sp, dc in next dc, ch 1, dc in next ch-1 sp, ch 1, tr in last tr; finish off: 18 sts and 9 sps.

ASSEMBLY

With Variegated, holding bottom edge of one Motif to top edge of next Motif, and using Placement Diagram as a guide, whipstitch Motifs together *(Fig. 10a, page 94)*, working through **both** loops of each st on **both** pieces and beginning in center ch of first corner ch-3 and ending in center ch of next corner ch-3, forming 5 vertical strips of 7 Motifs each; having bottom edges at same end, whipstitch strips together in same manner.

With Variegated, whipstitch a Square into each open area between Motifs, matching center ch of each corner ch-3 on Square to Motif joining.

With Variegated and using Placement Diagram as a guide, whipstitch Triangles to Afghan edges, matching tr on Triangle to center ch of corner ch-3 on Motif and center ch of ch-3 on Triangle to Motif joining.

PLACEMENT DIAGRAM

EDGING

Rnd 1: With **right** side facing, join Variegated with dc in first ch-3 sp on top corner Motif; ch 3, dc in same sp, ★ † ch 1, dc in next ch-1 sp, ch 1, (skip next dc, dc in next dc, ch 1, dc in next ch-1 sp, ch 1) twice, (dc, ch 3, dc) in next ch-3 sp, ch 1, dc in next ch-1 sp, ch 1, (skip next dc, dc in next dc, ch 1, dc in next ch-1 sp, ch 1) twice, ♥ dc in next sp, ch 1, skip next joining; working around dc at end of rows across Triangle, sc in first row, ch 1, (sc, ch 1) twice in next row, sc in next row, ch 1, hdc in free loop of beginning ch *(Fig. 2b, page 91)*, ch 1, sc in next row, ch 1, (sc, ch 1) twice in next row, sc in last row, ch 1, skip next joining, (dc in next sp, ch 1) twice, (skip next dc, dc in next dc, ch 1, dc in next ch-1 sp, ch 1) twice ♥; repeat from ♥ to ♥ across to next ch-3 sp †, (dc, ch 3, dc) in ch-3 sp; repeat from ★ 2 times **more**, then repeat from † to † once; join with slip st to first dc: 376 sps.

Rnd 2: (Slip st, ch 1, sc, ch 2, sc) in next ch-3 sp, ch 1, (sc in next ch-1 sp, ch 1) 6 times, ★ (sc, ch 2, sc) in next ch-3 sp, ch 1, (sc in next ch-1 sp, ch 1) across to next ch-3 sp; repeat from ★ around; join with slip st to first sc.

Rnd 3: (Slip st in next sp, ch 2) around; join with slip st to first slip st, finish off.

Design by Anne Halliday. ●

pink posies

Finished Size: 36" x 34" (91.5 cm x 86.5 cm)

MATERIALS
Light Weight Yarn
[5 ounces, 395 yards
(140 grams, 361 meters) per skein]:
  3 skeins
Crochet hook, size G (4 mm) **or** size needed
  for gauge
Ribbon roses - 4
Yarn needle
Sewing needle and thread

GAUGE: 20 dc and 11 rows = 5" (12.75 cm)

Gauge Swatch: 5" (12.75 cm) square
Ch 22.
Row 1: Dc in fourth ch from hook **(3 skipped chs count as first dc)** and in each ch across: 20 dc.
Rows 2-11: Ch 3 **(counts as first dc)**, turn; dc in next dc and in each dc across.
Finish off.

STITCH GUIDE

CLUSTER (uses one ch-1 sp)
★ YO, insert hook in ch-1 sp indicated, YO and pull up a loop, YO and draw through 2 loops on hook; repeat from ★ 2 times **more**, YO and draw through all 4 loops on hook.

AFGHAN BODY
Ch 151; place marker in third ch from hook for st placement.

Row 1: Dc in fourth ch from hook **(3 skipped chs count as first dc)** and in next 3 chs, ★ ch 2, skip next 2 chs, sc in next ch, ch 1, skip next 2 chs, (dc, ch 1) 3 times in next ch, skip next 2 chs, sc in next ch, ch 2, skip next 2 chs, dc in next 5 chs; repeat from ★ across: 95 sts and 54 sps.

Row 2 (Right side)**:** Ch 3 **(counts as first dc, now and throughout)**, turn; dc in next 4 dc, ★ skip next ch-2 sp, work Cluster in next ch-1 sp, (ch 3, work Cluster in next ch-1 sp) 3 times, skip next ch-2 sp, dc in next 5 dc; repeat from ★ across: 86 sts and 27 ch-3 sps.

Note: Loop a short piece of yarn around any stitch to mark Row 2 as **right** side.

Row 3: Ch 3, turn; dc in next 4 dc, ★ ch 2, sc in next ch-3 sp, (ch 3, sc in next ch-3 sp) twice, ch 2, skip next Cluster, dc in next 5 dc; repeat from ★ across: 77 sts and 36 sps.

Row 4: Ch 3, turn; dc in next 4 dc, ★ ch 5, skip next ch-2 sp, sc in next ch-3 sp, ch 3, sc in next ch-3 sp, ch 5, skip next ch-2 sp, dc in next 5 dc; repeat from ★ across: 68 sts and 27 sps.

Row 5: Ch 3, turn; dc in next 4 dc, ★ ch 2, sc in next ch-5 sp, ch 1, (dc, ch 1) 3 times in next ch-3 sp, sc in next ch-5 sp, ch 2, dc in next 5 dc; repeat from ★ across: 95 sts and 54 sps.

Row 6: Ch 3, turn; dc in next 4 dc, ★ skip next ch-2 sp, work Cluster in next ch-1 sp, (ch 3, work Cluster in next ch-1 sp) 3 times, skip next ch-2 sp, dc in next 5 dc; repeat from ★ across: 86 sts and 27 ch-3 sps.

Rows 7-71: Repeat Rows 3-6, 16 times; then repeat Row 3 once **more**; do **not** finish off: 77 sts and 36 sps.

BORDER

Rnd 1: Ch 1, turn; (sc, ch 3) twice in first dc, † (skip next dc, sc in next dc, ch 3) twice, (sc in next sp, ch 3) 4 times, sc in next dc, ch 3 †; repeat from † to † across to last 4 dc, skip next dc, sc in next dc, ch 3, skip next dc, (sc, ch 3) twice in last dc; working in end of rows, sc in same row, ch 3, (sc in next row, ch 3) across; working in free loops of beginning ch *(Fig. 2b, page 91)*, (sc, ch 3) twice in marked ch, ★ (skip next ch, sc in next ch, ch 3) twice, (sc in next sp, ch 3) 4 times, sc in ch at base of next dc, ch 3; repeat from ★ across to last 4 chs, skip next ch, sc in next ch, ch 3, skip next ch, (sc, ch 3) twice in last ch; working in end of rows, sc in same row, ch 3, (sc in next row, ch 3) across; join with slip st to first sc.

Rnds 2-7: Slip st in first corner ch-3 sp, ch 1, (sc, ch 3) twice in same sp, ★ (sc in next ch-3 sp, ch 3) across to next corner ch-3 sp, (sc, ch 3) twice in corner ch-3 sp; repeat from ★ 2 times **more**, (sc in next ch-3 sp, ch 3) across; join with slip st to first sc.

Finish off.

Using photo as a guide for placement, sew a ribbon rose in each corner of Afghan Body.

Design by Sandra Abbate. ●

soft as **snow**

Finished Size: 36" x 47" (91.5 cm x 119.5 cm)

MATERIALS
Medium Weight Yarn **4**
[3.5 ounces, 200 yards
(100 grams, 182 meters) per skein]:
   8 skeins
Crochet hook, size H (5 mm) **or** size needed
   for gauge
Yarn needle

GAUGE SWATCH: 3¾" (9.5 cm)
                  (straight edge to straight edge)
Work same as Motif.

STITCH GUIDE

TREBLE CROCHET (abbreviated tr)
YO twice, insert hook in st indicated, YO and pull
up a loop (4 loops on hook), (YO and draw through
2 loops on hook) 3 times.

MOTIF (Make 108)
Rnd 1 (Right side)**:** Ch 4, 2 dc in fourth ch from hook
(3 skipped chs count as first dc), ch 5, (3 dc in same
ch, ch 5) 3 times; join with slip st to first dc: 12 dc and
4 ch-5 sps.

Note: Loop a short piece of yarn around any stitch to
mark Rnd 1 as **right** side.

Rnd 2: Ch 3 **(counts as first dc, now and
throughout)**, dc in next 2 dc, ch 3, sc in next ch-5 sp,
ch 3, ★ dc in next 3 dc, ch 3, sc in next ch-5 sp, ch 3;
repeat from ★ 2 times **more**; join with slip st to first dc:
12 dc, 4 sc, and 8 ch-3 sps.

Rnd 3: Ch 3, dc in next 2 dc, ch 3, sc in next ch-3 sp, sc
in next sc and in next ch-3 sp, ch 3, ★ dc in next 3 dc,
ch 3, sc in next ch-3 sp, sc in next sc and in next ch-3 sp,
ch 3; repeat from ★ 2 times **more**; join with slip st to
first dc, finish off: 12 dc, 12 sc, and 8 ch-3 sps.

SQUARE (Make 88)
Rnd 1 (Right side)**:** Ch 4, 2 dc in fourth ch from hook
(3 skipped chs count as first dc), ch 3, (3 dc in same
ch, ch 3) 3 times; join with slip st to first dc, finish off:
12 dc and 4 ch-3 sps.

Note: Mark Rnd 1 as **right** side.

TRIANGLE (Make 38)
Row 1 (Right side)**:** Ch 6, 3 dc in sixth ch from hook
(5 skipped chs count as first tr plus ch 1), ch 3,
(3 dc, ch 1, tr) in same ch; finish off: 6 dc and 3 sps.

Note: Mark Row 1 as **right** side.

Instructions continued on page 57.

square flower

Finished Size: 37½" x 49½" (95.5 cm x 125.5 cm)

MATERIALS

Light Weight Yarn 🧶**LIGHT 3**

[1.75 ounces, 161 yards
(50 grams, 147 meters) per skein]:
   Yellow - 10 skeins
   Pink - 5 skeins
Crochet hook, size F (3.75 mm) **or** size needed
   for gauge
Tapestry needle

GAUGE: Each Square = 6" (15.25 cm)

Gauge Swatch: 2" (5 cm) square
With Pink, ch 10.
Row 1: Dc in fourth ch from hook (**3 skipped chs count as first dc**) and in each ch across: 8 dc.
Rows 2-4: Ch 3 (**counts as first dc**), turn; dc in next dc and in each dc across.
Finish off.

STITCH GUIDE

FRONT POST TREBLE CROCHET
   (abbreviated FPtr)
YO twice, insert hook from **front** to **back** around post of dc indicated (**Fig. 6, page 93**), YO and pull up a loop (4 loops on hook), (YO and draw through 2 loops on hook) 3 times.

SQUARE (Make 48)
FLOWER

FIRST SECTION
With Pink, ch 5; place marker in top 2 loops of second ch from hook (on First Section only) for Border placement (**Fig. 3b, page 92**).

Rows 1-4 are worked in Afghan Stitch with each row taking 2 steps, working to the **left** picking up loops and then working to the **right** completing each stitch (**Figs. 4a-c, page 92**).

Row 1 (Right side): Working from **right** to **left** in back ridge of beginning chs (**Fig. 3a, page 92**), pull up a loop in second ch from hook and in next 3 chs (5 loops on hook); working from **left** to **right**, YO and draw through first loop on hook, (YO and draw through 2 loops on hook) 4 times. One loop remains on hook. This is the first stitch of the next row.

Note: Loop a short piece of yarn around any stitch to mark Row 1 as **right** side.

Row 2: Working from **right** to **left**, skip first vertical strand, (insert hook under next vertical strand, YO and pull up a loop) 3 times, leave last vertical strand unworked (4 loops on hook); working from **left** to **right**, YO and draw through first loop on hook, (YO and draw through 2 loops on hook) 3 times.

Row 3: Working from **right** to **left**, skip first vertical strand, (insert hook under next vertical strand, YO and pull up a loop) twice, leave last vertical strand unworked (3 loops on hook); working from **left** to **right**, YO and draw through first loop on hook, (YO and draw through 2 loops on hook) twice.

Row 4: Working from **right** to **left**, skip first vertical strand, insert hook under next vertical strand, YO and pull up a loop, leave last vertical strand unworked (2 loops on hook); working from **left** to **right**, YO and draw through first loop on hook, YO and draw through both loops on hook; do **not** finish off.

Instructions continued on page 56.

continued from **square flower** page 54

NEXT 3 SECTIONS
Work same as First Section.

Drop loop from hook, with **right** side of First Section facing, being careful not to twist piece, and having tips to the inside, insert hook in first ch of beginning ch on First Section, hook dropped loop and draw through; finish off.

FLOWER CENTER

Rnd 1: With **right** side facing, join Yellow with slip st in marked st; skip next st, slip st in next st, ★ slip st in st before tip on next Section, skip next st, slip st in next st; repeat from ★ 2 times **more**: 8 slip sts.

Rnd 2: Working in Back Loops Only **(Fig. 1, page 91)**, slip st in first slip st, skip next slip st, (slip st in next slip st, skip next slip st) 3 times; finish off.

BORDER

Rnd 1: With **right** side facing and working in vertical strands at end of rows, join Yellow with sc in last row on any Section **(see Joining With Sc, page 91)**; 2 sc in same st, 3 sc in first row on next Section, sc in next 2 rows, ★ 3 sc in last row, 3 sc in first row on next Section, sc in next 2 rows; repeat from ★ 2 times **more**; join with slip st to Back Loop Only of first sc: 32 sc.

Rnd 2: Ch 3 **(counts as first dc)**, working in Back Loops Only, dc in next sc, 3 dc in next sc, ch 3, 3 dc in next sc, ★ dc in next 6 sc, 3 dc in next sc, ch 3, 3 dc in next sc; repeat from ★ 2 times **more**, dc in last 4 sc; join with slip st to **both** loops of first dc, finish off: 48 dc and 4 ch-3 sps.

Rnd 3: With **right** side facing, join Pink with dc in any corner ch-3 sp **(see Joining With Dc, page 91)**; (2 dc, ch 3, 3 dc) in same sp, dc in Back Loop Only of each dc around working (3 dc, ch 3, 3 dc) in each corner ch-3 sp; join with slip st to **both** loops of first dc, finish off: 72 dc and 4 ch-3 sps.

Rnd 4: With **right** side facing, join Yellow with dc in any corner ch-3 sp; (2 dc, ch 3, 3 dc) in same sp, ★ † ch 1, skip next dc, dc in Back Loop Only of next 4 dc, ch 1, skip next dc, work FPtr around dc on rnd **below** next dc, skip dc behind FPtr, dc in Back Loop Only of next 4 dc, work FPtr around dc on rnd **below** next dc, ch 1, skip dc behind FPtr and next dc, dc in Back Loop Only of next 4 dc, ch 1, skip next dc †, (3 dc, ch 3, 3 dc) in next corner ch-3 sp; repeat from ★ 2 times **more**, then repeat from † to † once; join with slip st to Back Loop Only of first dc, do **not** finish off: 80 sts and 20 sps.

Rnd 5: Ch 1, sc in Back Loop Only of each st and each ch around; join with slip st to **both** loops of first sc, finish off: 108 sc.

ASSEMBLY

With Yellow and working through **inside** loops only, whipstitch Squares together **(Fig. 10b, page 94)**, forming 6 vertical strips of 8 Squares each, beginning in first corner sc and ending in next corner sc; then whipstitch strips together in same manner.

EDGING

Rnd 1: With **right** side facing, join Yellow with slip st in any corner sc; ch 3, skip next sc, dc in next sc, (ch 2, skip next sc, slip st in next sc, ch 2, skip next sc, dc in next sc) 6 times, ★ † ch 2, slip st in next seam, ch 2, dc in next sc on next Square, (ch 2, skip next sc, slip st in next sc, ch 2, skip next sc, dc in next sc) 6 times †; repeat from † to † across to within one sc of next corner sc, ch 3, skip next sc, slip st in corner sc, ch 3, skip next sc, dc in next sc, (ch 2, skip next sc, slip st in next sc, ch 2, skip next sc, dc in next sc) 6 times; repeat from ★ 2 times **more**, then repeat from † to † across, dc in first slip st to form last ch-3 sp.

Rnd 2: Ch 6, slip st in next dc, ★ (ch 4, slip st in next dc) across to next corner, ch 6, slip st in next dc; repeat from ★ 2 times **more**, ch 4, (slip st in next dc, ch 4) across; join with slip st to last dc made on Rnd 1, finish off.

Design by Mary C. Abadir. ●

continued from **soft as snow** page 52

ASSEMBLY

Using Placement Diagram as a guide and working through **both** loops of each st on **both** pieces, whipstitch Motifs together *(Fig. 10a, page 94)*, forming 9 vertical strips of 12 Motifs each, beginning in center ch of first corner ch-3, working across 3-sc group and ending in center ch of next corner ch-3.

Whipstitch 11 Squares to first strip, matching dc and center ch of Square corners to center ch of Motif corners; then join to next strip. Continue joining strips and Squares in same manner.

Whipstitch Triangles to outer edges, matching corners.

PLACEMENT DIAGRAM

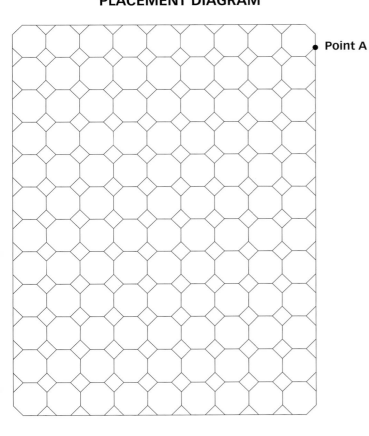

• Point A

EDGING

Rnd 1: With **right** side facing; join yarn with dc in first sc of 3-sc group at Point A *(see Joining With Dc, page 91)*; ★ † ch 1, skip next sc, dc in next sc, (ch 1, dc) twice in next ch-3 sp, place marker around last ch made for st placement, ch 1, dc in next dc, ch 1, skip next dc, dc in next dc, (ch 1, dc) twice in next ch-3 sp, place marker around last ch made for st placement, ch 1, [dc in next sc, ch 1, skip next sc, dc in next sc, ch 1, dc in center ch of next ch-3 (in joined corner), ch 1; working across next Triangle, sc around post of next tr, ch 1, hdc in center ch, ch 1, sc around post of next tr, ch 1, dc in center ch of next ch-3 (in joined corner), ch 1] across to last Motif on same side †, dc in next sc; repeat from ★ 2 times **more**, then repeat from † to † once; join with slip st to first dc.

Rnd 2: Ch 1, (sc in next ch-1 sp, ch 1) around moving markers to sc worked in marked sps; join with slip st to first sc.

Rnd 3: Ch 1, ★ (sc in next ch-1 sp, ch 1) across to next marked sc, sc in marked sc (remove marker), ch 1; repeat from ★ 7 times **more**, (sc in next ch-1 sp, ch 1) across; join with slip st to first sc.

Rnd 4: (Slip st in next ch-1 sp, ch 1) around; join with slip st to first slip st, finish off.

Design by Anne Halliday. ●

sonny boy

Finished Size: 29½" x 42" (75 cm x 106.5 cm)

MATERIALS

Light Weight Yarn
[5.6 ounces, 431 yards
(160 grams, 394 meters) per skein]:
   Blue - 3 skeins
   White - 2 skeins
Crochet hook, size H (5 mm) **or** size needed
   for gauge

GAUGE: In pattern, 8 Cross Sts and
   10 rows = 3¾" (9.5 cm)

Gauge Swatch: 4¼"w x 3¾"h (10.75 cm x 9.5 cm)
With White, ch 19.
Row 1: Working over Blue, sc in second ch from hook
and in each ch across changing to Blue in last sc
(Fig. 5b, page 93): 18 sc.
Row 2: Ch 3 **(counts as first dc)**, turn; working over
White, work Cross Sts across to last sc, dc in last sc
changing to White: 8 Cross Sts.
Row 3: Ch 1, turn; working over Blue, sc in each dc
across changing to Blue in last sc.
Rows 4-10: Repeat Rows 2 and 3, 3 times, then repeat
Row 2 once **more**; at end of Row 10, do **not** change to
White; finish off Blue and cut White.

STITCH GUIDE

CROSS STITCH (uses next 2 sts)
Skip next st, dc in next st, working **around** dc just
made, dc in skipped st.

AFGHAN BODY

With White, ch 127.

Row 1 (Right side)**:** Working over Blue, sc in second ch
from hook and in each ch across: 126 sc.

Note: Loop a short piece of yarn around any stitch to
mark Row 1 as **right** side.

Rows 2-8: Ch 1, turn; working over unused color, sc in
each sc across following Chart **(Figs. 5a & b, page 93)**.

Row 9: Ch 1, turn; working over Blue, sc in each sc
across changing to Blue in last sc.

Row 10: Ch 3 **(counts as first dc)**, turn; working over
White, work Cross Sts across to last sc, dc in last sc
changing to White: 62 Cross Sts.

Row 11: Ch 1, turn; working over Blue, sc in each dc
across changing to Blue in last sc.

Repeat Rows 10 and 11 for pattern until Afghan Body
measures approximately 39" (99 cm) from beginning ch,
ending by working Row 11; at end of last row, do **not**
change to Blue.

Repeat Rows 2-10 once; at end of last row, do **not**
change to White; finish off Blue and cut White.

CHART

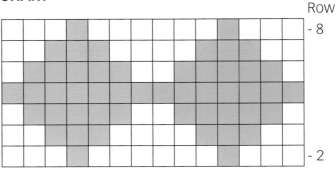

EDGING

Trim: With **wrong** side facing, working in free loops of beginning ch *(Fig. 2b, page 91)*, and working over White, join Blue with dc in ch at base of first sc *(see Joining With Dc, page 91)*; work Cross Sts across to last ch, dc in last ch changing to White: 62 Cross Sts.

Rnd 1: Ch 1, turn; working over Blue, ★ (sc, ch 1, sc) in first dc, sc in next dc and in each dc across to last dc, (sc, ch 1, sc) in last dc; working across end of rows, sc in each sc row and 2 sc in each dc row across; repeat from ★ once **more**; join with slip st to first sc, finish off White and cut Blue.

Design by Annis Clapp. •

spring **spirals**

Finished Size: 35" x 45" (89 cm x 114.5 cm)

MATERIALS

Medium Weight Yarn  **MEDIUM 4**
[3.5 ounces, 200 yards
(100 grams, 182 meters) per skein]:
 White - 7 skeins
 Blue - 2 skeins
 Pink - 2 skeins
Crochet hook, size H (5 mm) **or** size needed
 for gauge

GAUGE: In pattern, 5 Cross Sts and 8 rows = 4" (10 cm)

Gauge Swatch: 6"w x 4"h (15.25 cm x 10 cm)
With White, ch 26.
Rows 1-8: Work same as Afghan Body.
Finish off.

STITCH GUIDE

TREBLE CROCHET (abbreviated tr)
YO twice, insert hook in st indicated, YO and pull
up a loop (4 loops on hook), (YO and draw through
2 loops on hook) 3 times.

Each row is worked across length of Afghan.
When joining yarn and finishing off, always leave a
6" (15 cm) end to be worked into fringe.

AFGHAN BODY

With White, ch 170.

Row 1 (Right side): Sc in second ch from hook, ★ ch 1,
skip next ch, sc in next ch; repeat from ★ across;
finish off: 85 sc and 84 ch-1 sps.

Note: Loop a short piece of yarn around any stitch to
mark Row 1 as **right** side.

Row 2: With **wrong** side facing, join Blue with sc in first
sc **(see Joining With Sc, page 91)**; ch 4, skip next sc,
sc in next sc, drop Blue to **wrong** side and remove hook
from loop **(now and throughout)**; with **wrong** side
facing and working in **front** of ch-4, join Pink with sc in
skipped sc, ch 4, sc in next sc, ★ drop Pink to **wrong**
side; working in **front** of ch-4, insert hook in Blue loop,
ch 4, sc in next sc, drop Blue to **wrong** side; insert hook
in Pink loop, ch 4, sc in next sc; repeat from ★ across to
last sc, finish off Pink; insert hook in Blue loop, ch 4, sc in
last sc, finish off Blue.

Row 3: With **right** side facing, join White with sc in first
sc; ★ ch 1, working **behind** ch-4, sc in next sc; repeat
from ★ across: 85 sc and 84 ch-1 sps.

Row 4: Ch 4 **(counts as first dc plus ch 1, now and
throughout)**, turn; working in both loops of sc and in
top 2 loops of chs **(Fig. 3b, page 92)**, skip next 3 sts,
tr in next st, ch 1, working **behind** tr just made, tr in
second skipped st (counts as first Cross St), ★ skip next
2 sts, tr in next st, ch 1, working **behind** tr just made,
tr in first skipped st; repeat from ★ for each Cross St
across to last 2 sts, ch 1, skip next ch, dc in last sc:
55 Cross Sts.

Row 5: Ch 4, turn; ★ skip next tr, tr in next tr, ch 1,
working in **front** of tr just made, tr in skipped tr; repeat
from ★ for each Cross St across to last 2 sts, ch 1, skip
next ch, dc in last dc; finish off: 55 Cross Sts.

Row 6: With **wrong** side facing, join Blue with sc in first
dc; ch 4, working in both loops of tr and in top 2 loops
of chs, skip next 3 sts, sc in next tr, drop Blue to **wrong**
side; with **wrong** side facing and working in **front** of
ch-4, join Pink with sc in second skipped st, ch 4, skip
next st after Blue sc, sc in next st, ★ drop Pink to **wrong**
side; working in **front** of ch-4, insert hook in Blue loop,
ch 4, skip next st after Pink sc, sc in next st, drop Blue to
wrong side; insert hook in Pink loop, ch 4, skip next st
after Blue sc, sc in next st; repeat from ★ across to last
2 sts, finish off Pink; insert hook in Blue loop, ch 4, skip
next st, sc in last dc, finish off Blue.

Repeat Rows 3-6 for pattern until Afghan Body measures approximately 33½" (85 cm) from beginning ch, ending by working Row 3; do **not** finish off.

Next Row: Ch 1, turn; sc in first sc, (ch 1, sc in next sc) across.

Edging: Ch 1, turn; slip st in first sc and in next ch-1 sp, (ch 1, slip st in next ch-1 sp) across, slip st in last sc; finish off.

Beginning Edging: With **right** side facing and working in free loops of beginning ch *(Fig. 2b, page 91)* and in sps, join White with slip st in first ch; slip st in next ch-1 sp, (ch 1, slip st in next ch-1 sp) across, slip st in ch at base of last sc; finish off.

Holding 2 strands of corresponding color yarn together, each 12" (30.5 cm) long, add White and Blue fringe evenly spaced across short edges of Afghan Body *(Figs. 11a & b, page 94)*.

Design by Anne Halliday. ●

square motif with flower

Finished Size: 38" x 50" (96.5 cm x 127 cm)

MATERIALS
Light Weight Yarn (LIGHT 3)
[1.75 ounces, 161 yards
(50 grams, 147 meters) per skein]:
    Blue - 9 skeins
[2.5 ounces, 165 yards
(70 grams, 150 meters) per skein]:
    Green - 5 skeins
Crochet hook, size F (3.75 mm) **or** size needed
    for gauge
Tapestry needle

GAUGE: Each Square = 6" (15.25 cm)

Gauge Swatch: 2" (5 cm) square
With Green, ch 10.
Row 1: Dc in fourth ch from hook **(3 skipped chs count as first dc)** and in each ch across: 8 dc.
Rows 2-4: Ch 3 **(counts as first dc)**, turn; dc in next dc and in each dc across.
Finish off.

STITCH GUIDE

TREBLE CROCHET (abbreviated tr)
YO twice, insert hook in st indicated, YO and pull up a loop (4 loops on hook), (YO and draw through 2 loops on hook) 3 times.

SQUARE (Make 48)
CENTER
FIRST CORNER
With Green, ch 5; place marker in top 2 loops of last ch made (on First Corner only) for Border placement **(Fig. 3b, page 92)**.

Rows 1-4 are worked in Afghan Stitch with each row taking 2 steps, working to the **left** picking up loops and then working to the **right** completing each stitch **(Figs. 4a-c, page 92)**.

Row 1 (Right side)**:** Working from **right** to **left** in back ridge of beginning chs **(Fig. 3a, page 92)**, pull up a loop in second ch from hook and in next 3 chs (5 loops on hook); working from **left** to **right**, YO and draw through first loop on hook, (YO and draw through 2 loops on hook) 4 times. One loop remains on hook. This is the first stitch of the next row.

Note: Loop a short piece of yarn around any stitch to mark Row 1 as **right** side.

Row 2: Working from **right** to **left**, skip first vertical strand, (insert hook under next vertical strand, YO and pull up a loop) 3 times, leave last vertical strand unworked (4 loops on hook); working from **left** to **right**, YO and draw through first loop on hook, (YO and draw through 2 loops on hook) 3 times.

Row 3: Working from **right** to **left**, skip first vertical strand, (insert hook under next vertical strand, YO and pull up a loop) twice, leave last vertical strand unworked (3 loops on hook); working from **left** to **right**, YO and draw through first loop on hook, (YO and draw through 2 loops on hook) twice.

Row 4: Working from **right** to **left**, skip first vertical strand, insert hook under next vertical strand, YO and pull up a loop, leave last vertical strand unworked (2 loops on hook); working from **left** to **right**, YO and draw through first loop on hook, YO and draw through both loops on hook; do **not** finish off.

NEXT 2 CORNERS
Work same as First Corner.

LAST CORNER
Work same as First Corner through Row 3.

Row 4: Working from **right** to **left**, skip first vertical strand, insert hook under next vertical strand, YO and pull up a loop, leave last vertical strand unworked (2 loops on hook); YO and draw through first loop on hook, with **right** side of First Corner facing, being careful not to twist piece, and having tips on the outer edge, insert hook in first ch of beginning ch on First Corner, YO and draw through st and both loops on hook; finish off: 36 sts around outer edge.

FILL-IN MOTIF

With Blue, ch 5; join with slip st to form a ring.

Rnd 1: Ch 3, drop loop from hook, with **right** side of Center facing, insert hook from **top** to **bottom** in last unworked vertical strand on Row 2 of any Corner, ★ † hook dropped loop and draw through, ch 3, slip st in ring, ch 3, drop loop from hook, insert hook from **top** to **bottom** in last unworked vertical strand on Row 3 of same Corner, hook dropped loop and draw through, ch 3, slip st in ring †, ch 3, drop loop from hook, insert hook from **top** to **bottom** in unworked vertical strand on Row 2 of next Corner; repeat from ★ 2 times **more**, then repeat from † to † once; finish off.

Instructions continued on page 67.

grand **prize**

Finished Size: 36½" x 46½" (92.5 cm x 118 cm)

MATERIALS
Medium Weight Yarn
[3.5 ounces, 171 yards
(100 grams, 156 meters) per skein]:
  White - 4 skeins
  Scraps - 7 skeins **total**
Note: We used 6 different colors.
Crochet hook, size H (5 mm) **or** size needed
  for gauge
Yarn needle

GAUGE: Each Motif = 4" (10 cm)
             (straight edge to straight edge)

Gauge Swatch: 2½" (6.25 cm)
                 (straight edge to straight edge)
Work same as Motif through Rnd 2.

STITCH GUIDE

LONG SINGLE CROCHET *(abbreviated LSC)*
Working **around** same ch-2, insert hook in ch-2 sp
on Rnd 2 *(Fig. A)*, YO and pull up a loop even with
last sc made *(Fig. B)*, YO and draw through both
loops on hook.

Fig. A

Fig. B

MOTIF (Make 111)
With scrap color desired, ch 6; join with slip st to form
a ring.

Rnd 1 (Right side): Ch 3 **(counts as first dc, now and
throughout)**, dc in ring, ch 2, (2 dc in ring, ch 2) 5 times;
join with slip st to first dc: 12 dc and 6 ch-2 sps.

Note: Loop a short piece of yarn around any stitch to
mark Rnd 1 as **right** side.

Rnd 2: Ch 3, dc in next dc, (dc, ch 2, dc) in next ch-2 sp,
★ dc in next 2 dc, (dc, ch 2, dc) in next ch-2 sp; repeat
from ★ around; join with slip st to first dc: 24 dc and
6 ch-2 sps.

Rnd 3: Ch 3, dc in next 2 dc, (dc, ch 2, dc) in next
ch-2 sp, ★ dc in next 4 dc, (dc, ch 2, dc) in next ch-2 sp;
repeat from ★ around to last dc, dc in last dc; join with
slip st to first dc, finish off: 36 dc and 6 ch-2 sps.

Rnd 4: With **right** side facing, join White with sc in any
ch-2 sp **(see Joining With Sc, page 91)**; work LSC
(Figs. A & B), sc in same ch-2 sp on Rnd 3 and in next
6 dc, ★ (sc, work LSC, sc) in next ch-2 sp, sc in next
6 dc; repeat from ★ around; join with slip st to first sc,
finish off: 54 sts.

Instructions continued on page 66.

continued from **grand prize** page 64

ASSEMBLY

With White, using Placement Diagram as a guide, and working through **inside** loops only, whipstitch Motifs together *(Fig. 10b, page 94)*, forming 7 horizontal strips of 9 Motifs each and 6 horizontal strips of 8 Motifs each, beginning in first corner LSC and ending in next corner LSC, and arranging colors as desired; then whipstitch strips together in same manner.

PLACEMENT DIAGRAM

EDGING

With **right** side facing and working across short edge, join White with sc in third LSC on corner Motif; sc in same st, † sc in next 8 sc, sc in next joining and in next 8 sc, (2 sc in next LSC, sc in next 8 sc, sc in next joining and in next 8 sc) 7 times, (2 sc in next LSC, sc in next 8 sc) 3 times, [(sc in next joining and in next 8 sc) twice, (2 sc in next LSC, sc in next 8 sc) twice] 6 times †, 2 sc in next LSC, repeat from † to † once; join with slip st to first sc, finish off.

Design by Anita Kidd. ●

BORDER

Rnd 1: With **right** side of Center facing, join Blue with dc in marked ch **(see Joining With Dc, page 91)**; (dc, ch 2, 2 dc) in same st, dc in next 8 sts, ★ (2 dc, ch 2, 2 dc) in next corner st, dc in next 8 sts; repeat from ★ 2 times **more**; join with slip st to first dc, finish off: 48 dc and 4 ch-2 sps.

Rnd 2: With **right** side facing, join Green with dc in any corner ch-2 sp; (dc, ch 2, 2 dc) in same sp, ★ † dc in next dc, ch 1, (skip next dc, dc in next 2 dc, ch 1) 3 times, skip next dc, dc in next dc †, (2 dc, ch 2, 2 dc) in next corner ch-2 sp; repeat from ★ 2 times **more**, then repeat from † to † once; join with slip st to first dc, finish off: 48 dc and 20 sps.

Rnd 3: With **right** side facing, join Blue with dc in any corner ch-2 sp; (dc, ch 2, 2 dc) in same sp, ★ † dc in Back Loop Only of next 3 dc **(Fig. 1, page 91)**, working in front of next ch-1 **(Fig. 9, page 93)**, tr in **both** loops of skipped dc on Rnd 1, (dc in Back Loop Only of next 2 dc on Rnd 2, working in **front** of next ch-1, tr in **both** loops of next skipped dc on Rnd 1) 3 times, dc in Back Loop Only of next 3 dc on Rnd 2 †, (2 dc, ch 2, 2 dc) in next corner ch-2 sp; repeat from ★ 2 times **more**, then repeat from † to † once; join with slip st to **both** loops of first dc, do **not** finish off: 80 sts and 4 ch-2 sps.

Rnd 4: Ch 1, sc in both loops of same st and each st around working 3 sc in each corner ch-2 sp; join with slip st to first sc, finish off: 92 sc.

ASSEMBLY

With Blue and working through **inside** loops only, whipstitch Squares together **(Fig. 10b, page 94)**, forming 6 vertical strips of 8 Squares each, beginning in center sc of one corner 3-sc group and ending in center sc of next corner 3-sc group; then whipstitch strips together in same manner.

EDGING

Rnd 1: With **right** side facing, join Green with sc in center sc of any corner 3-sc group **(see Joining With Sc, page 91)**; ★ † ch 2, (skip next sc, sc in next sc, ch 1) 5 times, skip next 2 sc, sc in next sc, (ch 1, skip next sc, sc in next sc) 4 times, ch 2, [skip next sc, sc in next seam, ch 2, (skip next sc, sc in next sc, ch 1) 5 times, skip next 2 sc, sc in next sc, (ch 1, skip next sc, sc in next sc) 4 times, ch 2] across to next corner 3-sc group, skip next sc †, sc in next sc; repeat from ★ 2 times **more**, then repeat from † to † once; join with slip st to first sc, finish off.

Rnd 2: With **right** side facing, join Blue with sc in last ch-2 sp made; ch 1, sc in same sp, ch 1 (corner), (sc, ch 1) twice in next ch-2 sp, (sc in next ch-1 sp, ch 1) across to next ch-2 sp, ★ (sc, ch 1) twice in each of next 2 ch-2 sps, (sc in next ch-1 sp, ch 1) across to next ch-2 sp; repeat from ★ around; join with slip st to first sc, finish off.

Rnd 3: With **right** side facing, skip first ch-1 sp and join Green with sc in corner ch-1 sp; ch 2, sc in next ch-1 sp, (ch 1, sc in next ch-1 sp) across to next corner ch-1 sp, ★ (ch 2, sc in next ch-1 sp) twice, (ch 1, sc in next ch-1 sp) across to next corner ch-1 sp; repeat from ★ around, ch 2; join with slip st to first sc, finish off.

Rnd 4: With **right** side facing, join Blue with sc in last ch-2 sp made; ch 3, sc in next ch-2 sp, ch 2, sc in next ch-1 sp, (ch 1, sc in next ch-1 sp) across to next ch-2 sp, ch 2, ★ sc in next ch-2 sp, ch 3, sc in next ch-2 sp, ch 2, sc in next ch-1 sp, (ch 1, sc in next ch-1 sp) across to next ch-2 sp, ch 2; repeat from ★ around; join with slip st to first sc, finish off.

Design by Mary C. Abadir. ●

sweetest hearts

Finished Size: 39" x 53" (99 cm x 134.5 cm)

MATERIALS
Light Weight Yarn **3**
[5 ounces, 350 yards
(140 grams, 320 meters) per skein]:
    White - 4 skeins
    Pink - 2 skeins
Crochet hook, size G (4 mm) **or** size needed
    for gauge
Yarn needle
Safety pin

GAUGE: Each Square = 7" (17.75 cm)

Gauge Swatch: 3½" (9 cm) square
Work same as Square through Rnd 1 of Border.

STITCH GUIDE

TREBLE CROCHET (abbreviated tr)
YO twice, insert hook in dc indicated, YO and pull
up a loop (4 loops on hook), (YO and draw through
2 loops on hook) 3 times.
PICOT
Ch 2, hdc in second ch from hook.
CLUSTER
Ch 3, ★ YO, insert hook in third ch from hook, YO
and pull up a loop, YO and draw through 2 loops
on hook; repeat from ★ once **more**, YO and draw
through all 3 loops on hook.

SQUARE (Make 35)
HEART

Rnd 1 (Right side): With Pink, ch 2, 9 sc in second ch
from hook; join with slip st to first sc.

Note: Loop a short piece of yarn around any stitch to
mark Rnd 1 as **right** side.

Rnd 2: Ch 1, sc in same st and in next sc, ch 1, (dc, ch 1)
twice in next sc, (dc in next sc, ch 1) twice, (dc, ch 2,
dc) in next sc, ch 1, (dc in next sc, ch 1) twice, (dc, ch 1)
twice in last sc; join with slip st to first sc: 12 sts and
11 sps.

Rnd 3: Slip st in next sc, ch 1, dc in next dc, ch 1, (tr,
ch 1) 4 times in next dc, (dc in next dc, ch 1) 3 times,
(dc, ch 2, dc) in next ch-2 sp, ch 1, (dc in next dc, ch 1) 3
times, (tr, ch 1) 4 times in next dc, dc in next dc, ch 1,
place marker around ch-1 just made for st placement;
join with slip st to joining slip st: 19 sts and 19 sps.

Rnd 4: Work Picot, **turn**; (skip next ch-1 sp, slip st in
next st, work Picot) 8 times, skip next ch-1 sp, (slip st,
work Picot) twice in next ch-2 sp, skip next dc and next
ch-1 sp, slip st in next st, (work Picot, skip next ch-1 sp,
slip st in next st) 8 times; finish off: 19 Picots.

FILL-IN ROWS
Row 1: With **right** side facing, working **behind** Picots
and in sps on Rnd 3 **(Fig. 9, page 93)**, join White with
slip st in marked ch-1 sp; ch 5, slip st in next ch-1 sp,
ch 2, slip st in next ch-1 sp: 2 sps.

Row 2: Ch 2, turn; skip first ch-2 sp, (dc, ch 3, dc) in next
ch-5 sp, ch 2, working in **front** of next Picot, slip st in
next ch-1 sp on Rnd 3; do **not** finish off: 3 sps.

BORDER
Rnd 1: Ch 3 **(counts as first dc, now and
throughout)**, turn; dc in next ch-2 sp and in next dc,
(2 dc, ch 3, 2 dc) in next ch-3 sp, dc in next dc, 2 dc in
last ch-2 sp, ch 1, working **behind** Picots and in sps on
Rnd 3 of Heart, (sc in next ch-1 sp, ch 1) twice, (dc, ch 3,
dc) in next ch-1 sp, ch 1, dc in next ch-1 sp, ch 1, (hdc in
next ch-1 sp, ch 1) 3 times, (dc, ch 3, dc) in next ch-2 sp
(between slip sts), ch 1, (hdc in next ch-1 sp, ch 1) 3
times, dc in next ch-1 sp, ch 1, (dc, ch 3, dc) in next
ch-1 sp, ch 1, (sc in next ch-1 sp, ch 1) twice; join with
slip st to first dc: 28 sts and 20 sps.

Instructions continued on page 73.

story time

Finished Size: 52½" x 66½" (133.5 cm x 169 cm)

MATERIALS
Medium Weight Yarn

**[6 ounces, 312 yards
(170 grams, 285 meters) per skein]:**
    Purple - 5 skeins
    White - 4 skeins
Crochet hook, size H (5 mm) **or** size needed
    for gauge
Yarn needle

GAUGE: Each Motif = 7" (17.75 cm)
          (straight edge to straight edge)

Gauge Swatch: 4" (10 cm) diameter
Work same as Motif through Rnd 3.

STITCH GUIDE

TREBLE CROCHET (abbreviated tr)
YO twice, insert hook in st or sp indicated, YO and pull up a loop (4 loops on hook), (YO and draw through 2 loops on hook) 3 times.

BEGINNING CLUSTER (uses next 3 tr)
Ch 3, ★ YO twice, insert hook in **next** tr, YO and pull up a loop, (YO and draw through 2 loops on hook) twice; repeat from ★ 2 times **more**, YO and draw through all 4 loops on hook.

CLUSTER (uses next 4 tr)
★ YO twice, insert hook in **next** tr, YO and pull up a loop, (YO and draw through 2 loops on hook) twice; repeat from ★ 3 times **more**, YO and draw through all 5 loops on hook.

MOTIF (Make 63)

Rnd 1 (Right side): With White, ch 2, 8 sc in second ch from hook; join with slip st to first sc.

Note: Loop a short piece of yarn around any stitch to mark Rnd 1 as **right** side.

Rnd 2: Ch 3 **(counts as first dc)**, dc in same st, (ch 2, 2 dc in next sc) around, hdc in first dc to form last ch-2 sp: 16 dc and 8 ch-2 sps.

Rnd 3: Ch 4 **(counts as first tr)**, 3 tr in last ch-2 sp made, ch 1, (4 tr in next ch-2 sp, ch 1) around; join with slip st to first tr: 32 tr and 8 ch-1 sps.

Rnd 4: Work Beginning Cluster, ch 3, tr in next ch-1 sp, ch 3, ★ work Cluster, ch 3, tr in next ch-1 sp, ch 3; repeat from ★ around; join with slip st to top of Beginning Cluster, finish off: 8 Clusters and 16 ch-3 sps.

Rnd 5: With **right** side facing, join Purple with dc in any tr **(see Joining With Dc, page 91)**; 3 dc in next ch-3 sp, (dc, ch 1, dc) in next Cluster, 3 dc in next ch-3 sp, ★ dc in next tr, 3 dc in next ch-3 sp, (dc, ch 1, dc) in next Cluster, 3 dc in next ch-3 sp; repeat from ★ around; join with slip st to first dc, finish off: 72 dc and 8 ch-1 sps.

SQUARE (Make 48)

Rnd 1 (Right side): With Purple, ch 5, dc in fifth ch from hook **(4 skipped chs count as first dc plus ch 1)**, ch 3, ★ (dc, ch 1, dc) in same ch, ch 3; repeat from ★ 2 times **more**; join with slip st to first dc: 8 dc and 8 sps.

Note: Mark Rnd 1 as **right** side.

Rnd 2: Ch 4 **(counts as first dc plus ch 1)**, dc in next dc, ch 1, (dc, ch 3, dc) in next ch-3 sp, ch 1, ★ (dc in next dc, ch 1) twice, (dc, ch 3, dc) in next ch-3 sp, ch 1; repeat from ★ around; join with slip st to first dc, finish off: 16 dc and 16 sps.

TRIANGLE (Make 28)

With Purple, ch 5, place marker in second ch from hook for st placement; join with slip st to form a ring.

Row 1: Ch 5 **(counts as first tr plus ch 1, now and throughout Triangle)**, (dc, ch 1, dc, ch 3, dc, ch 1, dc) in ring, ch 1, tr in marked ch: 6 sts and 5 sps.

Row 2 (Right side)**:** Ch 5, turn; dc in next ch-1 sp, ch 1, (dc in next dc, ch 1) twice, (dc, ch 3, dc) in next ch-3 sp, ch 1, (dc in next dc, ch 1) twice, dc in next ch-1 sp, ch 1, tr in last tr; finish off: 10 sts and 9 sps.

Note: Mark Row 2 as **right** side.

Instructions continued on page 72.

continued from **story time** page 71

ASSEMBLY

With Purple, using Placement Diagram as a guide, and working through **both** loops, whipstitch Motifs together *(Fig. 10a, page 94)*, forming 7 vertical strips of 9 Motifs each, beginning in first corner ch and ending in next corner ch.

Whipstitch 8 Squares to first strip matching corner ch on Motif to center ch of corner ch-3 on Square; then whipstitch second strip to first strip. Continue joining Squares and strips in same manner.

Whipstitch Triangles to outer edges, beginning in first tr on Triangle and corresponding corner ch on Motif and ending in last tr on Triangle and corresponding corner ch on next Motif.

PLACEMENT DIAGRAM

EDGING

Rnd 1: With **right** side facing, join Purple with dc in first corner ch-1 sp on any corner Motif; ch 1, dc in next dc, ch 1, (skip next dc, dc in next dc, ch 1) 4 times, dc in next ch-1 sp, ch 1, dc in next dc, ch 1, (skip next dc, dc in next dc, ch 1) 4 times; ★ † working in end of rows on Triangle, sc in next row, ch 1, sc in top of next row, ch 1, sc in same row, ch 1, sc in free ch of ring, ch 1, sc in next row, ch 1, sc in top of same row, ch 1, sc in next row, ch 1; working across Motif, dc in next dc, ch 1, (skip next dc, dc in next dc, ch 1) 4 times †; repeat from † to † across to first corner ch of next corner Motif, dc in next ch-1 sp, place marker in dc just made for st placement, ch 1, dc in next dc, ch 1, (skip next dc, dc in next dc, ch 1) 4 times, dc in next ch-1 sp, ch 1, dc in next dc, ch 1, (skip next dc, dc in next dc, ch 1) 4 times; repeat from ★ 2 times **more**, then repeat from † to † across; join with slip st to first dc: 384 sts and 384 ch-1 sps.

Rnd 2: Ch 4 **(counts as first dc plus ch 1, now and throughout)**, dc in same st, ch 1, (dc in next dc, ch 1) 5 times, (dc, ch 1) twice in next dc, ★ (skip next ch, dc in next st, ch 1) across to next marked dc, (dc, ch 1, dc) in marked dc, remove marker and place in ch just made for st placement, ch 1, (dc in next dc, ch 1) 5 times, (dc, ch 1) twice in next dc; repeat from ★ 2 times **more**, (skip next ch, dc in next st, ch 1) across; join with slip st to first dc: 392 dc and 392 ch-1 sps.

Rnd 3: Ch 4, dc in next ch-1 sp, ch 1, (dc in next dc, ch 1) 7 times, dc in next ch-1 sp, ch 1, ★ (dc in next dc, ch 1) across to next marked ch, remove marker, dc in ch-1 sp, ch 1, (dc in next dc, ch 1) 7 times, dc in next ch-1 sp, ch 1; repeat from ★ 2 times **more**, (dc in next dc, ch 1) across; join with slip st to first dc: 400 dc and 400 ch-1 sps.

Rnd 4: (Slip st in next ch-1 sp, ch 1) around; join with slip st to first slip st, finish off.

Design by Anne Halliday. ●

continued from **sweetest hearts** page 68

Rnd 2: Ch 3, dc in next 4 dc, (2 dc, ch 3, 2 dc) in next corner ch-3 sp, dc in next 5 dc, (dc in next ch-1 sp and in next st) 3 times, (2 dc, ch 3, 2 dc) in next corner ch-3 sp, ★ dc in next dc, (dc in next ch-1 sp and in next st) across to next corner ch-3 sp, (2 dc, ch 3, 2 dc) in corner ch-3 sp; repeat from ★ once **more**, (dc in next st and in next ch-1 sp) 3 times; join with slip st to first dc, place loop from hook onto safety pin to keep piece from unraveling as you work the next rnd: 60 dc and 4 ch-3 sps.

Rnd 3: With **wrong** side facing, join Pink with sc in any corner ch-3 sp **(see Joining With Sc, page 91)**; work Cluster, sc in same sp, work Cluster, ★ skip next 3 dc, (sc in next dc, work Cluster, skip next 3 dc) 3 times, (sc, work Cluster) twice in next corner ch-3 sp; repeat from ★ 2 times **more**, skip next 3 dc, (sc in next dc, work Cluster, skip next 3 dc) across; join with slip st to first sc, finish off: 20 sc and 20 Clusters.

Rnd 4: With **right** side facing and working **behind** Clusters on Rnd 3, remove safety pin and place loop onto hook; ch 3, dc in next 2 dc on Rnd 2, sc in next sc on Rnd 3, dc in next 3 dc on Rnd 2, sc in next sc on Rnd 3, (dc, ch 3, dc) in next corner ch-3 sp on Rnd 2 (between sc), sc in next sc on Rnd 3, ★ (dc in next 3 dc on Rnd 2, sc in next sc on Rnd 3) 4 times, (dc, ch 3, dc) in next corner ch-3 sp on Rnd 2 (between sc), sc in next sc on Rnd 3; repeat from ★ 2 times **more**, (dc in next 3 dc on Rnd 2, sc in next sc on Rnd 3) twice; join with slip st to first dc: 76 sts and 4 ch-3 sps.

Rnd 5: Slip st in next dc, ch 4 **(counts as first dc plus ch 1, now and throughout)**, dc in same st, ch 1, skip next 3 sts, (dc, ch 1) twice in next dc, skip next 3 sts, (dc, ch 1, dc, ch 3, dc, ch 1, dc) in next corner ch-3 sp, ch 1, ★ skip next 3 sts, [(dc, ch 1) twice in next dc, skip next 3 sts] 4 times, (dc, ch 1, dc, ch 3, dc, ch 1, dc) in next corner ch-3 sp, ch 1; repeat from ★ 2 times **more**, skip next 3 sts, [(dc, ch 1) twice in next dc, skip next 3 sts] twice; join with slip st to first dc, finish off: 48 dc and 48 sps.

ASSEMBLY

With White and working through **both** loops of each st on **both** pieces, whipstitch Squares together forming 5 vertical strips of 7 Squares each **(Fig. 10a, page 94)**, beginning in center ch of first corner ch-3 and ending in center ch of next corner ch-3; then whipstitch strips together in same manner.

EDGING

Rnd 1: With **right** side facing, join White with dc in top right corner ch-3 sp **(see Joining With Dc, page 91)**; † ch 1, ★ [(dc, ch 1) twice in next ch-1 sp, skip next sp] 6 times, (dc, ch 1) twice in next joining, skip next sp; repeat from ★ 3 times **more**, (dc, ch 1) twice in next ch-1 sp, [skip next ch-1 sp, (dc, ch 1) twice in next ch-1 sp] 5 times, (dc, ch 3, dc) in next corner ch-3 sp, ch 1, ♥ [(dc, ch 1) twice in next ch-1 sp, skip next sp] 6 times, (dc, ch 1) twice in next joining, skip next sp ♥; repeat from ♥ to ♥ 5 times **more**, (dc, ch 1) twice in next ch-1 sp, [skip next ch-1 sp, (dc, ch 1) twice in next ch-1 sp] 5 times †, (dc, ch 3, dc) in next corner ch-3 sp, repeat from † to † once, dc in same sp as first dc, ch 2, sc in first dc to form last corner ch-3 sp: 336 sps.

Rnd 2: Ch 4, dc in last ch-3 sp made, ★ † ch 1, skip next ch-1 sp, [(dc, ch 1) twice in next ch-1 sp, skip next ch-1 sp] across to next corner ch-3 sp †, (dc, ch 1, dc, ch 3, dc, ch 1, dc) in corner ch-3 sp; repeat from ★ 2 times **more**, then repeat from † to † once, (dc, ch 1, dc) in same sp as first dc, ch 2, sc in first dc to form last ch-3 sp: 344 sps.

Rnd 3: Ch 1, sc in last ch-3 sp made, work Cluster, ch 1, skip next ch-1 sp, (sc in next ch-1 sp, work Cluster, ch 1, skip next ch-1 sp) across to next corner ch-3 sp, ★ (sc, work Cluster, ch 1) twice in corner ch-3 sp, skip next ch-1 sp, (sc in next ch-1 sp, work Cluster, ch 1, skip next ch-1 sp) across to next corner ch-3 sp; repeat from ★ 2 times **more**, sc in same sp as first sc, work Cluster, ch 1; join with slip st to first sc, finish off.

Design by Anne Halliday. ●

taffy

Finished Size: 38" x 51" (96.5 cm x 129.5 cm)

MATERIALS
Medium Weight Yarn 🔵**4**
[3.5 ounces, 216 yards
(100 grams, 197 meters) per skein]:
    10 skeins
Crochet hook, size I (5.5 mm) **or** size needed
    for gauge
Yarn needle

GAUGE: Each Motif = 6½" (16.5 cm)
        (straight edge to straight edge)
        Each Square = 3" (7.5 cm)

Gauge Swatch: 3" (7.5 cm) square
Work same as Square.

STITCH GUIDE

TREBLE CROCHET (abbreviated tr)
YO twice, insert hook in st or sp indicated, YO and
pull up a loop (4 loops on hook), (YO and draw
through 2 loops on hook) 3 times.
BEGINNING CLUSTER (uses next 3 dc)
Ch 2, ★ YO, insert hook in **next** dc, YO and pull up a
loop, YO and draw through 2 loops on hook; repeat
from ★ 2 times **more**, YO and draw through all
4 loops on hook.
CLUSTER (uses next 4 dc)
★ YO, insert hook in **next** dc, YO and pull up a loop,
YO and draw through 2 loops on hook; repeat from
★ 3 times **more**, YO and draw through all 5 loops
on hook.

MOTIF (Make 35)
Ch 6; join with slip st to form a ring.

Rnd 1 (Right side): Ch 3 (**counts as first dc, now and
throughout**), 3 dc in ring, ch 3, (4 dc in ring, ch 3) 3
times; join with slip st to first dc: 16 dc and 4 ch-3 sps.

Note: Loop a short piece of yarn around any stitch to
mark Rnd 1 as **right** side.

Rnd 2: Work Beginning Cluster, ch 3, 4 dc in next
ch-3 sp, ch 3, ★ work Cluster, ch 3, 4 dc in next ch-3 sp,
ch 3; repeat from ★ 2 times **more**; join with slip st to top
of Beginning Cluster: 20 sts and 8 ch-3 sps.

Rnd 3: Ch 6, dc in next ch-3 sp, ch 3, work Cluster, ch 3,
dc in next ch-3 sp, ch 3, ★ dc in next Cluster, ch 3, dc in
next ch-3 sp, ch 3, work Cluster, ch 3, dc in next ch-3 sp,
ch 3; repeat from ★ 2 times **more**; join with slip st to
third ch of beginning ch-6: 16 sts and 16 ch-3 sps.

Rnd 4: Slip st in next ch and in same ch-3 sp, ch 4, (dc,
ch 1) twice in next dc, ★ (dc in next ch-3 sp, ch 1) twice,
(dc, ch 1) twice in next dc; repeat from ★ around to last
ch-3 sp, dc in last ch-3 sp, ch 1; join with slip st to third
ch of beginning ch-4: 32 sts and 32 ch-1 sps.

Rnd 5: Ch 3, dc in next ch-1 sp and in next dc, (dc, ch 1,
dc) in next ch-1 sp, ★ dc in next dc, (dc in next ch-1 sp
and in next dc) 3 times, (dc, ch 1, dc) in next ch-1 sp;
repeat from ★ 6 times **more**, (dc in next dc and in next
ch-1 sp) twice; join with slip st to first dc, finish off: 72 dc
and 8 ch-1 sps.

SQUARE (Make 24)

Rnd 1 (Right side)**:** Ch 4, 2 dc in fourth ch from hook, ch 3, (3 dc in same ch, ch 3) 3 times; join with slip st to top of beginning ch-4: 12 sts and 4 ch-3 sps.

Note: Mark Rnd 1 as **right** side.

Rnd 2: Ch 3, dc in next 2 dc, (2 dc, ch 3, 2 dc) in next ch-3 sp, ★ dc in next 3 dc, (2 dc, ch 3, 2 dc) in next ch-3 sp; repeat from ★ 2 times **more**; join with slip st to first dc, finish off: 28 dc and 4 ch-3 sps.

TRIANGLE (Make 20)

Ch 6; join with slip st to form a ring.

Row 1: Ch 5 **(counts as first tr plus ch 1, now and throughout)**, (3 dc, ch 3, 3 dc, ch 1, tr) in ring: 8 sts and 3 sps.

Row 2 (Right side)**:** Ch 5, turn; 2 dc in next ch-1 sp, dc in next 3 dc, (2 dc, ch 3, 2 dc) in next ch-3 sp, dc in next 3 dc, 2 dc in next ch-1 sp, ch 1, tr in last tr; finish off.

Note: Mark Row 2 as **right** side.

Instructions continued on page 79.

sweetheart roses

■■□□ EASY +

Finished Size: 33" x 35" (84 cm x 89 cm)

MATERIALS

Light Weight Yarn
[5 ounces, 395 yards
(140 grams, 361 meters) per skein]:
Green - 3 skeins
Pink - 1 skein
Super Fine Weight Yarn
[1.75 ounces, 286 yards
(50 grams, 262 meters) per skein]:
Pink - 1 skein
Crochet hooks, sizes D (3.25 mm) **and** G (4 mm) **or**
sizes needed for gauge
Yarn needle

GAUGE: With Light Weight Yarn and larger size hook,
20 dc and 11 rows = 5" (12.75 cm)

Gauge Swatch: 3½" (9 cm)
(from straight edge to straight edge)
Work same as Motif.

STITCH GUIDE

BEGINNING POPCORN (uses one st)
Ch 3 **(counts as first dc)**, work 3 dc in st indicated,
drop loop from hook, insert hook in first dc of
4-dc group, hook dropped loop and draw through.
POPCORN (uses one sc)
Work 4 dc in sc indicated, drop loop from hook,
insert hook in first dc of 4-dc group, hook dropped
loop and draw through.
BEGINNING CLUSTER (uses one sp)
Ch 2, ★ YO, insert hook in **same** sp, YO and pull up a
loop, YO and draw through 2 loops on hook; repeat
from ★ once **more**, YO and draw through all 3 loops
on hook.
CLUSTER (uses one sp)
★ YO, insert hook in sp indicated, YO and pull up a
loop, YO and draw through 2 loops on hook; repeat
from ★ 2 times **more**, YO and draw through all
4 loops on hook.

Use Light Weight Yarn and larger size hook throughout
Afghan unless otherwise specified.

MOTIF (Make 94)

Rnd 1 (Right side)**:** With Pink, ch 2, 6 sc in second ch
from hook; join with slip st to first sc.

Note: Loop a short piece of yarn around any stitch to
mark Rnd 1 as **right** side.

Rnd 2: Work Beginning Popcorn in same st, ch 3, (work
Popcorn in next sc, ch 3) around; join with slip st to
top of Beginning Popcorn, finish off: 6 Popcorns and
6 ch-3 sps.

Rnd 3: With **right** side facing, join Green with slip st
in any ch-3 sp; work (Beginning Cluster, ch 3, Cluster)
in same sp, ch 1, ★ work (Cluster, ch 3, Cluster) in next
ch-3 sp, ch 1; repeat from ★ around; join with slip st to
top of Beginning Cluster: 12 Clusters and 12 sps.

Rnd 4: Slip st in first ch-3 sp, ch 3 **(counts as first dc, now and throughout)**, (2 dc, ch 2, 3 dc) in same sp, ch 1, 3 dc in next ch-1 sp, ch 1, ★ (3 dc, ch 2, 3 dc) in next ch-3 sp, ch 1, 3 dc in next ch-1 sp, ch 1; repeat from ★ around; join with slip st to first dc, finish off: 54 dc and 18 sps.

HALF MOTIF (Make 10)

Row 1: With Pink, ch 2, 5 sc in second ch from hook; do **not** join.

Row 2 (Right side): Ch 4 **(counts as first dc plus ch 1, now and throughout)**, turn; work Popcorn in next sc, (ch 3, work Popcorn in next sc) twice, ch 1, dc in last sc; finish off: 4 sps.

Note: Mark Row 2 as **right** side.

Row 3: With **wrong** side facing, join Green with slip st in first dc; ch 4, work Cluster in next ch-1 sp, ch 1, [work (Cluster, ch 3, Cluster) in next ch-3 sp, ch 1] twice, work Cluster in next ch-1 sp, ch 1, dc in last dc: 6 Clusters, 2 dc, and 7 sps.

Row 4: Ch 4, turn; (3 dc in next ch-1 sp, ch 1) twice, (3 dc, ch 2, 3 dc) in next ch-3 sp, ch 1, 3 dc in next ch-1 sp, ch 1, (3 dc, ch 2, 3 dc) in next ch-3 sp, ch 1, (3 dc in next ch-1 sp, ch 1) twice, dc in last dc; finish off: 29 dc and 10 sps.

Instructions continued on page 78.

ASSEMBLY

With Green, using Placement Diagram as a guide, and working through **inside** loops of each st on **both** pieces, whipstitch Motifs and Half Motifs together **(Fig. 10b, page 94)**, forming 6 horizontal strips of 9 Motifs each and 5 horizontal strips of 8 Motifs and 2 Half Motifs each, beginning in second ch of first ch-2 and ending in first ch of next ch-2; then whipstitch strips together in same manner.

PLACEMENT DIAGRAM

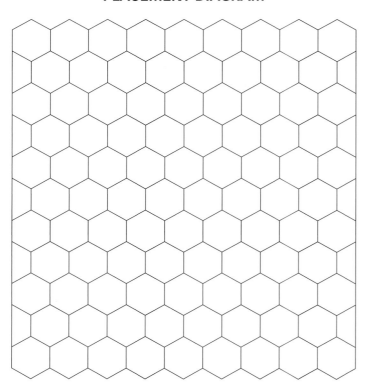

TRIM

First Side: With **right** side facing and working across long edge of Afghan, join Green with sc in first dc after corner ch-2 sp **(see Joining With Sc, page 91)**; sc in next 2 dc, (skip next ch-1 sp, sc in next 3 dc) twice, ★ skip next joining, working across end of rows on Half Motif, 2 sc in each of next 3 rows, sc in side of next 2 sc on Row 1, 2 sc in each of next 3 rows, skip next joining, sc in next 3 dc, (skip next ch-1 sp, sc in next 3 dc) twice; repeat from ★ 4 times **more**; finish off.

Second Side: Work same as First Side.

Edging: With **right** side facing and using smaller size hook, join Pink Super Fine Weight Yarn with sc in first sc on either Side; ch 3, † (sc in next sc, ch 3) across; [skip next sp, (sc in next dc, ch 3) 3 times] 6 times, ★ skip next joining, (sc in next dc, ch 3) 3 times, [skip next sp, (sc in next dc, ch 3) 3 times] 5 times; repeat from ★ 7 times **more**, skip next ch-2 sp †; repeat from † to † once **more**; join with slip st to first sc, finish off.

Design by Sandra Abbate. ●

continued from **taffy** page 75

ASSEMBLY

Using Placement Diagram as a guide and working through **both** loops of each st on **both** pieces, whipstitch Motifs together forming 5 vertical strips of 7 Motifs each **(Fig. 10a, page 94)**, beginning in ch of first corner and ending in ch of next corner. Whipstitch 6 Squares to first strip matching ch of Motif corners to center ch of Square corner; then whipstitch second strip to first strip. Continue joining strips and Squares in same manner. Whipstitch Triangles to outer edges beginning in first tr on Triangle and corresponding ch on Motif and ending in last tr on Triangle and corresponding ch on next Motif.

PLACEMENT DIAGRAM

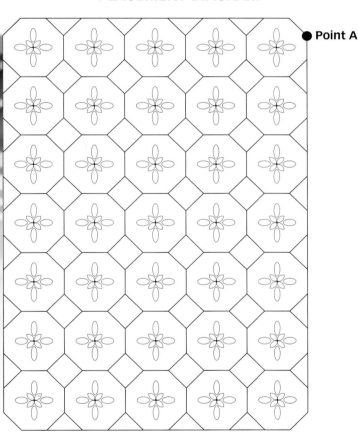

● Point A

EDGING

Rnd 1: With **right** side facing, join yarn with slip st in ch-1 sp at Point A; ch 3, ★ † 2 dc in next dc, dc in next 7 dc, 2 dc in next dc, dc in next ch-1 sp, 2 dc in next dc, dc in next 8 dc, ch 1; working in end of rows on Triangle, sc in next row, ch 1, sc in top of next row, ch 1, sc in same row, ch 1, sc in ring, ch 1, sc in next row, ch 1, sc in top of same row, ch 1, sc in next row, ch 1, [working across Motif, dc in next 9 dc, ch 1, working in end of rows on Triangle, sc in next row, ch 1, sc in top of next row, ch 1, sc in same row, ch 1, sc in ring, ch 1, sc in next row, ch 1, sc in top of same row, ch 1, sc in next row, ch 1] across to last Motif, dc in next 8 dc, 2 dc in next dc †, dc in next ch-1 sp, place marker in dc just made for st placement; repeat from ★ 2 times **more**, then repeat from † to † once; join with slip st to first dc: 416 sts and 160 ch-1 sps.

Rnd 2: Ch 4 **(counts as first dc plus ch 1, now and throughout)**, dc in same st, (ch 1, skip next dc, dc in next dc) 6 times, place marker in last dc made for st placement, ch 1, dc in same st, ch 1, skip next dc, ★ (dc in next st, ch 1, skip next dc or ch) across to next marked dc, dc in marked dc, remove marker, place marker in dc just made for st placement, ch 1, dc in same st, (ch 1, skip next dc, dc in next dc) 6 times, place marker in last dc made for st placement, ch 1, dc in same st, ch 1, skip next dc; repeat from ★ 2 times **more**, (dc in next st, ch 1, skip next dc or ch) across; join with slip st to first dc: 296 dc and 296 ch-1 sps.

Rnd 3: Ch 3, dc in same st and in next ch-1 sp, 2 dc in next dc, dc in next ch-1 sp, ★ (dc in next dc and in next ch-1 sp) across to next marked dc, 2 dc in marked dc, remove marker, dc in next ch-1 sp, place marker in dc just made for st placement, 2 dc in next dc, dc in next ch-1 sp; repeat from ★ 6 times **more**, (dc in next dc and in next ch-1 sp) across; join with slip st to first dc: 608 dc.

Rnd 4: Ch 4, skip next dc, (dc, ch 1) twice in next dc, skip next dc, ★ (dc in next dc, ch 1, skip next dc) across to next marked dc, (dc, ch 1) twice in marked dc, skip next dc; repeat from ★ 6 times **more**, (dc in next dc, ch 1, skip next dc) across; join with slip st to first dc.

Rnd 5: (Slip st in next ch-1 sp, ch 1) around; join with slip st to first slip st, finish off.

Design by Anne Halliday. ●

tender hearts

Finished Size: 36" x 46½" (91.5 cm x 118 cm)

MATERIALS

Light Weight Yarn **LIGHT 3**
[1.75 ounces, 180 yards
(50 grams, 165 meters) per skein]:
   9 skeins
Crochet hook, size G (4 mm) **or** size needed
   for gauge

GAUGE: In pattern, 15 sts and 8 rows = 4" (10 cm)

Gauge Swatch: 4" (10 cm) square
Ch 17.
Row 1 (Right side)**:** Dc in third ch from hook (**3 skipped chs count as first dc**) and in each ch across: 15 dc.
Rows 2-8: Ch 3 (**counts as first dc, now and throughout**), turn; dc in next dc and in each dc across. Finish off.

AFGHAN BODY

Ch 133; place marker in third ch from hook for st placement.

Row 1 (Right side)**:** Dc in fourth ch from hook (**3 skipped chs count as first dc**) and in next 25 chs, ★ ch 1, skip next ch, (dc in next ch, ch 1, skip next ch) 12 times, dc in next 27 chs; repeat from ★ once **more**: 105 dc and 26 ch-1 sps.

Row 2: Ch 3 (**counts as first dc, now and throughout**), turn; dc in next 26 dc, ★ ch 1, (dc in next dc, ch 1) 12 times, dc in next 27 dc; repeat from ★ once **more**.

Row 3: Ch 3, turn; dc in next 12 dc, ch 1, skip next dc, dc in next 13 dc, ★ (ch 1, dc in next dc) 6 times, dc in next ch-1 sp, (dc in next dc, ch 1) 6 times, dc in next 13 dc, ch 1, skip next dc, dc in next 13 dc; repeat from ★ once **more**: 104 dc and 27 ch-1 sps.

Row 4: Ch 3, turn; dc in next 10 dc, ch 1, skip next dc, (dc in next dc, ch 1) twice, skip next dc, dc in next 11 dc, ★ (ch 1, dc in next dc) 5 times, dc in next ch-1 sp, dc in next 3 dc and in next ch-1 sp, (dc in next dc, ch 1) 5 times, dc in next 11 dc, ch 1, skip next dc, (dc in next dc, ch 1) twice, skip next dc, dc in next 11 dc; repeat from ★ once **more**: 102 dc and 29 ch-1 sps.

Row 5: Ch 3, turn; dc in next 8 dc, ch 1, skip next dc, (dc in next dc, ch 1) 4 times, skip next dc, dc in next 9 dc, ★ (ch 1, dc in next dc) 4 times, dc in next ch-1 sp, dc in next 7 dc and in next ch-1 sp, (dc in next dc, ch 1) 4 times, dc in next 9 dc, ch 1, skip next dc, (dc in next dc, ch 1) 4 times, skip next dc, dc in next 9 dc; repeat from ★ once **more**: 100 dc and 31 ch-1 sps.

Row 6: Ch 3, turn; dc in next 6 dc, ch 1, skip next dc, (dc in next dc, ch 1) 6 times, skip next dc, dc in next 7 dc, ★ (ch 1, dc in next dc) 3 times, dc in next ch-1 sp, dc in next 11 dc and in next ch-1 sp, (dc in next dc, ch 1) 3 times, dc in next 7 dc, ch 1, skip next dc, (dc in next dc, ch 1) 6 times, skip next dc, dc in next 7 dc; repeat from ★ once **more**: 98 dc and 33 ch-1 sps.

Row 7: Ch 3, turn; dc in next 4 dc, ch 1, skip next dc, (dc in next dc, ch 1) 8 times, skip next dc, dc in next 5 dc, ★ (ch 1, dc in next dc) twice, dc in next ch-1 sp, dc in next 15 dc and in next ch-1 sp, (dc in next dc, ch 1) twice, dc in next 5 dc, ch 1, skip next dc, (dc in next dc, ch 1) 8 times, skip next dc, dc in next 5 dc; repeat from ★ once **more**: 96 dc and 35 ch-1 sps.

Instructions continued on page 82.

Row 8: Ch 3, turn; dc in next 4 dc, ch 1, (dc in next dc, ch 1) 8 times, dc in next 5 dc, ★ ch 1, dc in next dc, ch 1, dc in next 19 dc, ch 1, dc in next dc, ch 1, dc in next 5 dc, ch 1, (dc in next dc, ch 1) 8 times, dc in next 5 dc; repeat from ★ once **more**.

Row 9: Ch 3, turn; dc in next 4 dc, (ch 1, dc in next dc) 4 times, dc in next ch-1 sp, (dc in next dc, ch 1) 4 times, dc in next 5 dc, ★ ch 1, dc in next dc, ch 1, dc in next 9 dc, ch 1, skip next dc, dc in next 9 dc, ch 1, dc in next dc, ch 1, dc in next 5 dc, (ch 1, dc in next dc) 4 times, dc in next ch-1 sp, (dc in next dc, ch 1) 4 times, dc in next 5 dc; repeat from ★ once **more**: 97 dc and 34 ch-1 sps.

Row 10: Ch 3, turn; dc in next 4 dc, ★ † dc in next ch-1 sp and in next dc, (ch 1, dc in next dc) twice, dc in next ch-1 sp and in next 3 dc, dc in next ch-1 sp and in next dc, (ch 1, dc in next dc) twice, dc in next ch-1 sp and in next 5 dc †, ch 1, (dc in next dc, ch 1) twice, [skip next dc, dc in next 5 dc, ch 1, skip next dc, (dc in next dc, ch 1) twice] 2 times, dc in next 5 dc; repeat from ★ once **more**, then repeat from † to † once: 101 dc and 30 ch-1 sps.

Row 11: Ch 3, turn; dc in next 6 dc, (dc in next ch-1 sp and in next dc, dc in next ch-1 sp and in next 7 dc) twice, ★ [(ch 1, dc in next dc) 3 times, (ch 1, skip next dc, dc in next dc) twice] 2 times, ch 1, (dc in next dc, ch 1) twice, dc in next 7 dc, (dc in next ch-1 sp and in next dc, dc in next ch-1 sp and in next 7 dc) twice; repeat from ★ once **more**: 105 dc and 26 ch-1 sps.

Rows 12 and 13: Ch 3, turn; dc in next 26 dc, ★ ch 1, (dc in next dc, ch 1) 12 times, dc in next 27 dc; repeat from ★ once **more**.

Row 14: Ch 4 **(counts as first dc plus ch 1, now and throughout)**, turn; skip next dc, dc in next dc, (ch 1, skip next dc, dc in next dc) 12 times, ★ (dc in next ch-1 sp and in next dc) 13 times, (ch 1, skip next dc, dc in next dc) 13 times; repeat from ★ once **more**: 92 dc and 39 ch-1 sps.

Row 15: Ch 4, turn; (dc in next dc, ch 1) 12 times, dc in next 27 dc, ch 1, (dc in next dc, ch 1) 12 times, dc in next 27 dc, (ch 1, dc in next dc) 13 times.

Row 16: Ch 4, turn; dc in next dc, (ch 1, dc in next dc) 5 times, ★ dc in next ch-1 sp, (dc in next dc, ch 1) 6 times, dc in next 13 dc, ch 1, skip next dc, dc in next 13 dc, (ch 1, dc in next dc) 6 times; repeat from ★ once **more**, dc in next ch-1 sp and in next dc, (ch 1, dc in next dc) 6 times: 93 dc and 38 ch-1 sps.

Row 17: Ch 4, turn; ★ † (dc in next dc, ch 1) 4 times, dc in next dc and in next ch-1 sp, dc in next 3 dc and in next ch-1 sp, (dc in next dc, ch 1) 5 times †, dc in next 11 dc, ch 1, skip next dc, (dc in next dc, ch 1) twice, skip next dc, dc in next 11 dc, ch 1; repeat from ★ once **more**, then repeat from † to † once, dc in last dc: 95 dc and 36 ch-1 sps.

Row 18: Ch 4, turn; ★ † (dc in next dc, ch 1) 3 times, dc in next dc and in next ch-1 sp, dc in next 7 dc and in next ch-1 sp, (dc in next dc, ch 1) 4 times †, dc in next 9 dc, ch 1, skip next dc, (dc in next dc, ch 1) 4 times, skip next dc, dc in next 9 dc, ch 1; repeat from ★ once **more**, then repeat from † to † once, dc in last dc: 97 dc and 34 ch-1 sps.

Row 19: Ch 4, turn; ★ † (dc in next dc, ch 1) twice, dc in next dc and in next ch-1 sp, dc in next 11 dc and in next ch-1 sp, (dc in next dc, ch 1) 3 times †, dc in next 7 dc, ch 1, skip next dc, (dc in next dc, ch 1) 6 times, skip next dc, dc in next 7 dc, ch 1; repeat from ★ once **more**, then repeat from † to † once, dc in last dc: 99 dc and 32 ch-1 sps.

Row 20: Ch 4, turn; ★ † dc in next dc, ch 1, dc in next dc and in next ch-1 sp, dc in next 15 dc and in next ch-1 sp, (dc in next dc, ch 1) twice †, dc in next 5 dc, ch 1, skip next dc, (dc in next dc, ch 1) 8 times, skip next dc, dc in next 5 dc, ch 1; repeat from ★ once **more**, then repeat from † to † once, dc in last dc: 101 dc and 30 ch-1 sps.

Row 21: Ch 4, turn; dc in next dc, ch 1, dc in next 19 dc, ★ ch 1, dc in next dc, ch 1, dc in next 5 dc, ch 1, (dc in next dc, ch 1) 8 times, dc in next 5 dc, ch 1, dc in next dc, ch 1, dc in next 19 dc; repeat from ★ once **more**, (ch 1, dc in next dc) twice.

Row 22: Ch 4, turn; ★ † dc in next dc, ch 1, dc in next 9 dc, ch 1, skip next dc, dc in next 9 dc, ch 1, dc in next dc, ch 1 †, dc in next 5 dc, (ch 1, dc in next dc) 4 times, dc in next ch-1 sp, (dc in next dc, ch 1) 4 times, dc in next 5 dc, ch 1; repeat from ★ once **more**, then repeat from † to † once, dc in last dc: 100 dc and 31 ch-1 sps.

Row 23: Ch 4, turn; ★ † (dc in next dc, ch 1) twice, [skip next dc, dc in next 5 dc, ch 1, skip next dc, (dc in next dc, ch 1) twice] 2 times †, dc in next 5 dc and in next ch-1 sp, (dc in next dc, ch 1) twice, dc in next dc and in next ch-1 sp, dc in next 3 dc, dc in next ch-1 sp and in next dc, (ch 1, dc in next dc) twice, dc in next ch-1 sp and in next 5 dc, ch 1; repeat from ★ once **more**, then repeat from † to † once, dc in last dc: 96 dc and 35 ch-1 sps.

Row 24: Ch 4, turn; ★ † (dc in next dc, ch 1) twice, [(dc in next dc, ch 1, skip next dc) twice, (dc in next dc, ch 1) 3 times] twice †, dc in next 7 dc, (dc in next ch-1 sp and in next dc, dc in next ch-1 sp and in next 7 dc) twice, ch 1; repeat from ★ once **more**, then repeat from † to † once, dc in last dc: 92 dc and 39 ch-1 sps.

Rows 25 and 26: Ch 4, turn; (dc in next dc, ch 1) 12 times, dc in next 27 dc, ch 1, (dc in next dc, ch 1) 12 times, dc in next 27 dc, (ch 1, dc in next dc) 13 times.

Row 27: Ch 3, turn; (dc in next ch-1 sp and in next dc) 13 times, ★ (ch 1, skip next dc, dc in next dc) 13 times, (dc in next ch-1 sp and in next dc) 13 times; repeat from ★ once **more**: 105 dc and 26 ch-1 sps.

Rows 28-91: Repeat Rows 2-27 twice, then repeat Rows 2-13 once **more**; at end of Row 91, do **not** finish off.

EDGING

Rnd 1: Ch 1, do **not** turn; working in end of rows, sc in first dc on Row 91, ch 1, (sc in top of next row, ch 1) across; working in free loops of beginning ch *(Fig. 2b, page 91)*, (sc, ch 2, sc) in first ch, sc in next ch and in each ch across to marked ch, (sc, ch 2, sc) in marked ch, ch 1; working in end of rows, sc in top of first row, ch 1, (sc in top of next row, ch 1) across to last row, skip last row; working across Row 91, (sc, ch 2, sc) in first dc, sc in each dc and in each ch across, sc in same st as first sc, hdc in first sc to form last corner ch-2 sp: 446 sc and 186 sps.

Rnd 2: Ch 1, (sc, ch 2, sc) in last ch-2 sp made, † sc in next sc, (ch 1, sc in next sc) across to next corner ch-2 sp, (sc, ch 2, sc) in corner ch-2 sp †, sc in each sc across to next corner ch-2 sp, (sc, ch 2, sc) in corner ch-2 sp, repeat from † to † once, sc in each sc across; join with slip st to first sc: 454 sc and 186 sps.

Rnd 3: Ch 2, slip st in next corner ch-2 sp, † ch 1, slip st in next sc, ch 1, (slip st in next ch-1 sp, ch 1) across to within 2 sc of next corner ch-2 sp, skip next sc, slip st in next sc, ch 1, slip st in next corner ch-2 sp, ch 2, slip st in next sc, ch 2 †, (skip next sc, slip st in next sc, ch 2) across to next corner ch-2 sp, slip st in corner ch-2 sp, repeat from † to † once, (skip next sc, slip st in next sc, ch 2) across to last sc, skip last sc; join with slip st to joining slip st, finish off.

Design by Anne Halliday. ●

starlight **star bright**

Finished Size: 33½" x 44" (85 cm x 112 cm)

MATERIALS

Medium Weight Yarn
[3 ounces, 150 yards
(85 grams, 137 meters) per skein]:
  Variegated - 4 skeins
[3½ ounces, 171 yards
(100 grams, 156 meters) per skein]:
  Yellow - 4 skeins
  Blue - 3 skeins
Crochet hook, size H (5 mm) **or** size needed
  for gauge
Yarn needle

GAUGE SWATCH: 3½" (9 cm) square
Work same as Solid Square.

STITCH GUIDE

TREBLE CROCHET (abbreviated tr)
YO twice, insert hook in sp indicated, YO and pull
up a loop (4 loops on hook), (YO and draw through
2 loops on hook) 3 times.

BEGINNING CLUSTER (uses one sp)
Ch 2, ★ YO, insert hook in sp indicated, YO and pull
up a loop, YO and draw through 2 loops on hook;
repeat from ★ once **more**, YO and draw through all
3 loops on hook.

CLUSTER (uses one sp)
★ YO, insert hook in sp indicated, YO and pull up a
loop, YO and draw through 2 loops on hook; repeat
from ★ 2 times **more**, YO and draw through all
4 loops on hook.

WRAPPED DC (uses 2 sps)
YO, insert hook in sp indicated, YO and pull up a loop,
insert hook in **next** sp indicated, YO and pull up a
loop (4 loops on hook), YO and draw through 3 loops
on hook, YO and draw through 2 loops on hook.

CROSS ST (uses next 2 sts)
Skip next st, dc in next st, working **around** dc just
made, dc in skipped st.

When finishing off each Square, leave end long enough to
sew two sides together.

SOLID SQUARE (Make 12)
With Yellow, ch 4; join with slip st to form a ring.

Rnd 1 (Right side)**:** Work Beginning Cluster in ring, ch 3,
(work Cluster in ring, ch 3) 4 times; join with slip st to top
of Beginning Cluster: 5 Clusters and 5 ch-3 sps.

Note: Loop a short piece of yarn around any stitch to
mark Rnd 1 as **right** side.

Rnd 2: Ch 3 **(counts as first hdc plus ch 1)**, (hdc, ch 1)
3 times in next ch-3 sp, (hdc, ch 1) 4 times in each of
next 4 ch-3 sps; join with slip st to first hdc: 20 hdc and
20 ch-1 sps.

Rnd 3: Slip st in next ch-1 sp, ch 4 **(counts as first tr,
now and throughout)**, 2 dc in same sp, ch 1, skip next
ch-1 sp, 3 dc in next ch-1 sp, ch 1, skip next ch-1 sp, (2 dc,
tr) in next ch-1 sp, ch 3, ★ (tr, 2 dc) in next ch-1 sp, ch 1,
skip next ch-1 sp, 3 dc in next ch-1 sp, ch 1, skip next
ch-1 sp, (2 dc, tr) in next ch-1 sp, ch 3; repeat from ★
2 times **more**; join with slip st to first tr, finish off: 36 sts
and 12 sps.

Instructions continued on page 88

wavy strips

Finished Size: 38½" x 51¼" (98 cm x 130 cm)

MATERIALS

Light Weight Yarn 【LIGHT 3】

[7 ounces, 575 yards
(198 grams, 525 meters) per skein]:
  Lavender - 2 skeins
  Green - 2 skeins
  White - 1 skein
Crochet hook, size G (4 mm) **or** size needed
  for gauge
Yarn needle

GAUGE: 2 repeats (40 sts) = 10¼" (26 cm)

Gauge Swatch: 10¼" x 3" (26 cm x 7.5 cm)
With Green, ch 42.
Work same as Strip A.

> Each row is worked across length of Strip.
> When joining yarn and finishing off, leave a 6"
> (15 cm) length to be worked into fringe.

STITCH GUIDE

TREBLE CROCHET (abbreviated tr)
YO twice, insert hook in st or sp indicated, YO
and pull up a loop (4 loops on hook), (YO and
draw through 2 loops on hook) 3 times.
CLUSTER
Ch 4, sc in second ch from hook, 2 dc in next
ch, sc in last ch (4-st row made); fold row in
half from **right** to **left**, slip st in skipped ch at
edge of first sc made.

STRIP A (Make 9)
FIRST HALF
With Green, ch 202.

Row 1 (Right side)**:** Sc in second ch from hook, ch 1, skip
next ch, sc in next ch, ★ † ch 1, skip next ch, hdc in next ch,
ch 1, skip next ch, dc in next ch, ch 1, skip next ch, tr in next
ch, ch 1, skip next ch, (tr, ch 1) twice in next ch, skip next ch,
tr in next ch, ch 1, skip next ch, dc in next ch, ch 1, skip next
ch, hdc in next ch, ch 1, skip next ch, sc in next ch †, (work
Cluster, skip next ch, sc in next ch) twice; repeat from ★
8 times **more**, then repeat from † to † once, ch 1, skip next
ch, sc in last ch: 31 sc, 20 hdc, 20 dc, 40 tr, 18 Clusters, and
92 chs.

Note: Loop a short piece of yarn around last sc made to
mark **right** side and top edge.

Row 2: Ch 1, turn; keeping Clusters to **right** side, sc in first
sc, (ch 1, skip next ch, sc in next st) 5 times, ch 1, sc in next
ch, ch 1, sc in next tr, ★ (ch 1, skip next ch or Cluster, sc
in next st) 10 times, ch 1, sc in next ch, ch 1, sc in next tr;
repeat from ★ across to last 10 sts, (ch 1, skip next ch, sc in
next st) 5 times; finish off: 121 sc and 120 chs.

Row 3: With **right** side facing, join White with sc in first sc
(see Joining With Sc, page 91); ★ ch 1, skip next ch, sc in
next sc; repeat from ★ across; finish off.

SECOND HALF
Row 1: With **right** side of First Half facing and working in
free loops of beginning ch **(Fig. 2b, page 91)**, join Green
with sc in first ch; ch 1, skip next ch, sc in next ch, ★ † ch 1,
skip next ch, hdc in next ch, ch 1, skip next ch, dc in next ch,
ch 1, skip next ch, tr in next ch, ch 1, skip next ch, (tr, ch 1)
twice in next ch, skip next ch, tr in next ch, ch 1, skip next
ch, dc in next ch, ch 1, skip next ch, hdc in next ch, ch 1,
skip next ch, sc in next ch †, (work Cluster, skip next ch, sc
in next ch) twice; repeat from ★ 8 times **more**, then repeat
from † to † once, ch 1, skip next ch, sc in last ch: 31 sc,
20 hdc, 20 dc, 40 tr, 18 Clusters, and 92 chs.

Rows 2 and 3: Work same as First Half of Strip A.

STRIP B (Make 8)
FIRST HALF
With Lavender, ch 205.

Row 1 (Right side)**:** Tr in fifth ch from hook **(4 skipped chs count as first tr)**; ch 1, ★ † skip next ch, tr in next ch, ch 1, skip next ch, dc in next ch, ch 1, skip next ch, hdc in next ch, ch 1, skip next ch, sc in next ch, (work Cluster, skip next ch, sc in next ch) twice, ch 1, skip next ch, hdc in next ch, ch 1, skip next ch, dc in next ch, ch 1, skip next ch, tr in next ch, ch 1, skip next ch †, (tr, ch 1) twice in next ch; repeat from ★ 8 times **more**, then repeat from † to † once, 2 tr in last ch: 30 sc, 20 hdc, 20 dc, 42 tr, 20 Clusters, and 89 chs.

Note: Loop a short piece of yarn around last tr made to mark **right** side and top edge.

Instructions continued on page 88.

continued from **wavy strips** page 87

Row 2: Ch 1, turn; keeping Clusters to **right** side, sc in first tr, ch 1, sc in next tr, (ch 1, skip next ch or Cluster, sc in next st) 10 times, ★ ch 1, sc in next ch, ch 1, sc in next tr, (ch 1, skip next ch or Cluster, sc in next st) 10 times; repeat from ★ across to last tr, ch 1, sc in last tr; finish off: 121 sc and 120 chs.

Row 3: With **right** side facing, join White with sc in first sc; ★ ch 1, skip next ch, sc in next sc; repeat from ★ across; finish off.

SECOND HALF

Row 1: With **right** side facing and working in free loops of beginning ch, join Lavender with slip st in first ch; ch 4 **(counts as first tr)**, tr in same ch as joining, ch 1, ★ † skip next ch, tr in next ch, ch 1, skip next ch, dc in next ch, ch 1, skip next ch, hdc in next ch, ch 1, skip next ch, sc in next ch, (work Cluster, skip next ch, sc in next ch) twice, ch 1, skip next ch, hdc in next ch, ch 1, skip next ch, dc in next ch, ch 1, skip next ch, tr in next ch, ch 1, skip next ch †, (tr, ch 1) twice in next ch; repeat from ★ 8 times **more**, then repeat from † to † once, 2 tr in next ch: 30 sc, 20 hdc, 20 dc, 42 tr, 20 Clusters, and 89 chs.

Rows 2 and 3: Work same as First Half of Strip B.

ASSEMBLY

Afghan is assembled by joining Strips in the following order: Strip A, (Strip B, Strip A) 8 times.

Join Strips as follows:
With White, having top edges at same end and working through **both** loops of each st on **both** pieces, whipstitch Strips together **(Fig. 10a, page 94)** across long edge.

EDGING

With **right** side of long edge facing, join White with slip st in first sc on Row 3; (slip st in next ch-1 sp, ch 1) across to last sc, slip st in last sc; finish off.

Repeat across opposite long edge.

Holding 2 strands of corresponding color yarn together, each 24" (61 cm) long, add additional fringe evenly across short edges of Afghan **(Figs. 11a & b, page 94)**.

Design by Anne Halliday. ●

continued from **starlight star bright** page 84

TRIANGLE SQUARE (Make 96)
Make 48 Variegated & Yellow and 48 Variegated & Blue.

Note: To change colors, drop old color and pick up new color, YO and pull through loop on hook **(color change ch made)**; do **not** carry yarn not in use.

With color indicated, ch 4; join with slip st to form a ring.

Rnd 1 (Right side): Ch 3 **(counts as first dc, now and throughout)**, (2 dc, ch 2, 3 dc) in ring, ch 1; with next color ch 1, (3 dc in ring, ch 2) twice; join with slip st to first dc: 12 dc and 4 sps.

Rnd 2: Turn; (slip st, ch 3, dc) in next ch-2 sp, ch 2, hdc in center dc of next 3-dc group, ch 2, (2 dc, ch 2, 2 dc) in next ch-2 sp, ch 2, hdc in next dc of next 3-dc group, ch 2, 2 dc in next ch-2 sp, ch 1; with next color ch 1, 2 dc in same sp, ch 2, hdc in center dc of next 3-dc group, ch 2, (2 dc, ch 2, 2 dc) in next ch-2 sp, ch 2, hdc in center dc of next 3-dc group, ch 2, 2 dc in first ch-2 sp, ch 2; join with slip st to first dc: 20 sts and 12 sps.

Rnd 3: Turn; (slip st, ch 3, 2 dc) in next ch-2 sp, ch 1, dc in next ch-2 sp, work Wrapped dc in same sp and in next ch-2 sp, dc in same sp for last leg of Wrapped dc, ch 1, (3 dc, ch 3, 3 dc) in next ch-2 sp, ch 1, dc in next ch-2 sp, work Wrapped dc in same sp and in next ch-2 sp, dc in same sp for last leg of Wrapped dc, ch 1, 3 dc in next ch-2 sp, ch 2; with next color ch 1, 3 dc in same sp, ch 1, dc in next ch-2 sp, work Wrapped dc in same sp and in next ch-2 sp, dc in same sp for last leg of Wrapped dc, ch 1, (3 dc, ch 3, 3 dc) in next ch-2 sp, ch 1, dc in next ch-2 sp, work Wrapped dc in same sp and in next ch-2 sp, dc in same sp for last leg of Wrapped dc, ch 1, 3 dc in first ch-2 sp, ch 3; join with slip st to first dc, finish off: 36 sts and 12 sps.

ASSEMBLY

With matching yarn, using Placement Diagram as a guide, and working through **inside** loops of each st on **both** pieces, whipstitch Squares together *(Fig. 10b, page 94)* forming 12 horizontal strips of 9 Squares each, beginning in center ch of first corner ch-3 and ending in center ch of next corner ch-3; then whipstitch strips together in same manner.

EDGING

Rnd 1: With **right** side facing and working in Back Loops Only *(Fig. 1, page 91)*, join Yellow with sc in center ch of any corner ch-3 *(see Joining With Sc, page 91)*; sc in each st and ch around entire Afghan, skipping seams where Squares join, except for one extra sc at top and bottom edges of Afghan for an even number of sc, and working (sc, ch 1, sc) in each center corner ch, ending with sc in first center corner ch, ch 1; join with slip st to first sc, finish off: 556 sc and 4 sps.

Rnd 2: With **right** side facing and working in both loops, join Variegated with dc in first sc of Rnd 1 *(see Joining With Dc, page 91)*; work Cross Sts around entire Afghan, working an extra Cross St at corners by working in same st twice; join with slip st to first dc, finish off: 282 Cross Sts.

Rnd 3: With **right** side facing, join Blue with sc in any corner; sc in each dc around entire Afghan, working 2 sc in each of 2 corner dc; join with slip st to first sc, finish off.

Design by Annis Clapp. ●

PLACEMENT DIAGRAM

KEY

– Yellow Solid Squares

– Yellow & Variegated Triangle Squares

– Blue & Variegated Triangle Squares

general instructions

ABBREVIATIONS

BPdc	Back Post double crochet(s)
ch(s)	chain(s)
cm	centimeters
dc	double crochet(s)
FP	Front Post
FPdc	Front Post double crochet(s)
FPsc	Front post single crochet(s)
FPtr	Front Post treble crochet(s)
hdc	half double crochet(s)
LSC	Long Single Crochet(s)
mm	millimeters
Rnd(s)	Round(s)
sc	single crochet(s)
sp(s)	space(s)
st(s)	stitch(es)
tr	treble crochet(s)
YO	yarn over

★ — work instructions following ★ as many **more** times as indicated in addition to the first time.

† to † or ♥ to ♥ — work all instructions from first † to second † or from first ♥ to second ♥ **as many** times as specified.

( ) or [ ] — work enclosed instructions **as many** times as specified by the number immediately following **or** work all enclosed instructions in the stitch or space indicated **or** contains explanatory remarks.

colon (:) — the number(s) given after a colon at the end of a row or round denote(s) the number of stitches or spaces you should have on that row or round.

GAUGE

Exact gauge is essential for proper size. Before beginning your Afghan, make the sample swatch given in the individual instructions in the yarn and hook specified. After completing the swatch, measure it, counting your stitches and rows or rounds carefully. If your swatch is larger or smaller than specified, **make another, changing hook size to get the correct gauge**. Keep trying until you find the size hook that will give you the specified gauge.

CROCHET TERMINOLOGY	
UNITED STATES	**INTERNATIONAL**
slip stitch (slip st) =	single crochet (sc)
single crochet (sc) =	double crochet (dc)
half double crochet (hdc) =	half treble crochet (htr)
double crochet (dc) =	treble crochet (tr)
treble crochet (tr) =	double treble crochet (dtr)
double treble crochet (dtr) =	triple treble crochet (ttr)
triple treble crochet (tr tr) =	quadruple treble crochet (qtr)
skip =	miss

Yarn Weight Symbol & Names	LACE 0	SUPER FINE 1	FINE 2	LIGHT 3	MEDIUM 4	BULKY 5	SUPER BULKY 6
Type of Yarns in Category	Fingering, 10-count crochet thread	Sock, Fingering Baby	Sport, Baby	DK, Light Worsted	Worsted, Afghan, Aran	Chunky, Craft, Rug	Bulky, Roving
Crochet Gauge* Ranges in Single Crochet to 4" (10 cm)	32-42 double crochets**	21-32 sts	16-20 sts	12-17 sts	11-14 sts	8-11 sts	5-9 sts
Advised Hook Size Range	Steel*** 6,7,8 Regular hook B-1	B-1 to E-4	E-4 to 7	7 to I-9	I-9 to K-10.5	K-10.5 to M-13	M-13 and larger

*GUIDELINES ONLY: The chart above reflects the most commonly used gauges and hook sizes for specific yarn categories.

** Lace weight yarns are usually crocheted on larger-size hooks to create lacy openwork patterns. Accordingly, a gauge range is difficult to determine. Always follow the gauge state in your pattern.

*** Steel crochet hooks are sized differently from regular hooks–the higher the number the smaller the hook, which is the reverse of regular hook sizing.

CROCHET HOOKS												
U.S.	B-1	C-2	D-3	E-4	F-5	G-6	H-8	I-9	J-10	K-10½	N	P	Q
Metric - mm	2.25	2.75	3.25	3.5	3.75	4	5	5.5	6	6.5	9	10	15

MARKERS

Markers are used to help distinguish the beginning of each round being worked. Place a 2" (5 cm) scrap piece of yarn before the first stitch of each round, moving the marker after each round is complete.

JOINING WITH SC

When instructed to join with sc, begin with a slip knot on the hook. Insert the hook in the stitch or space indicated, YO and pull up a loop, YO and draw through both loops on hook.

JOINING WITH HDC

When instructed to join with a hdc, begin with a slip knot on the hook. YO, holding loop on the hook, insert the hook in the stitch or space indicated, YO and pull up a loop, YO and draw through all 3 loops on hook.

JOINING WITH DC

When instructed to join with a dc, begin with a slip knot on the hook. YO, holding loop on the hook, insert the hook in the stitch or space indicated, YO and pull up a loop (3 loops on hook), (YO and draw through 2 loops on hook) twice.

BACK OR FRONT LOOP ONLY

Work only in loop(s) indicated by arrow *(Fig. 1)*.

Fig. 1

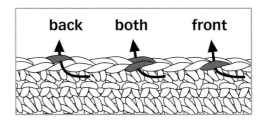

FREE LOOPS

After working in Back or Front Loops Only on a row or round, there will be a ridge of unused loops. These are called the free loops. Later, when instructed to work in the free loops of the same row or round, work in these loops *(Fig. 2a)*.

When instructed to work in free loops of a chain, work in the loop indicated by arrow *(Fig. 2b)*.

Fig. 2a   **Fig. 2b**

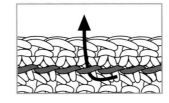 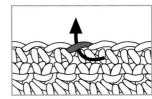

◖◻◻◻ BEGINNER	Projects for first-time crocheters using basic stitches. Minimal shaping.
◖◼◻◻ EASY	Projects using yarn with basic stitches, repetitive stitch patterns, simple color changes, and simple shaping and finishing.
◖◼◼◻ INTERMEDIATE	Projects using a variety of techniques, such as basic lace patterns or color patterns, mid-level shaping and finishing.
◖◼◼◗ EXPERIENCED	Projects with intricate stitch patterns, techniques and dimension, such as non-repeating patterns, multi-color techniques, fine threads, small hooks, detailed shaping and refined finishing.

WORKING INTO A CHAIN

Method 1: Work only in back ridge indicated by arrows *(Fig. 3a)*.

Fig. 3a

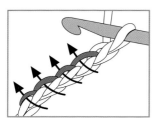

Method 2: Insert hook in top 2 loops (opposite back ridge) as indicated by arrows *(Fig. 3b)*.

Fig. 3b

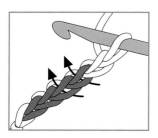

Method 3: Holding chain with back ridge to the back, insert hook under top loop and back ridge as indicated by arrows *(Fig. 3c)*.

Fig. 3c

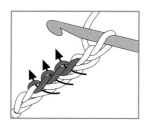

AFGHAN STITCH
FIRST ROW

Working from **right** to **left** in back ridge of beginning chs *(Fig. 3a)*, insert hook in second ch from hook, YO and pull up a loop (2 loops on hook), (insert hook in next ch, YO and pull up a loop) across *(Fig. 4a)*; working from **left** to **right**, YO and draw through first loop on hook, ★ YO and draw through 2 loops on hook *(Fig. 4b)*; repeat from ★ across. One loop remains on hook. This is the first stitch of the next row.

Fig. 4a

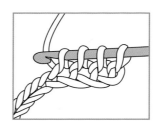

Fig. 4b

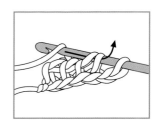

NEXT ROW

Working from **right** to **left**, skip first vertical strand, ★ insert hook under next vertical strand *(Fig. 4c)*, YO and pull up a loop; repeat from ★ across as many times as specified; working from **left** to **right**, YO and draw through first loop on hook, (YO and draw through 2 loops on hook) across.

Fig. 4c

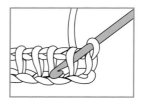

CHANGING COLORS

Insert hook in stitch indicated, YO and pull up a loop, drop yarn, with new yarn *(Figs. 5a & b)*, YO and draw through both loops on hook. Work over unused yarn until next color change.

Fig. 5a

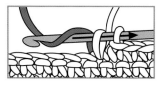

Fig. 5b

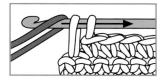

POST STITCH

Work around post of stitch indicated, inserting hook in direction of arrow *(Fig. 6)*.

Fig. 6

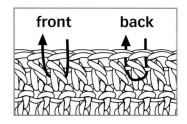

WORKING IN TOP OF A STITCH

When instructed to work into the top of a stitch just made, insert hook in direction of arrow *(Fig. 7)*.

Fig. 7

WORKING IN A SPACE BEFORE A STITCH

When instructed to work in space **before** a stitch of in spaced **between** stitches, insert hook in space indicated by arrow *(Fig. 8)*.

Fig. 8

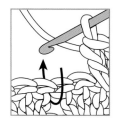

WORKING IN FRONT OF, AROUND, OR BEHIND A STITCH

Work in stitch or space indicated, inserting hook in direction of arrow *(Fig. 9)*.

Fig. 9

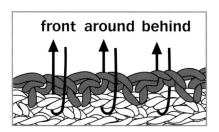

WHIPSTITCH

Place two Motifs, Squares, or Strips with **wrong** sides together. Sew through both pieces once to secure the beginning of the seam, leaving an ample yarn end to weave in later. Insert the needle from **front** to **back** through **both** loops of each stitch on **both** pieces **or** through **inside** loops only of each stitch on **both** pieces *(Figs. 10a or b)*. Bring the needle around and insert it from front to back through next loops of both pieces. Continue in this manner across, keeping the sewing yarn fairly loose.

Fig. 10a

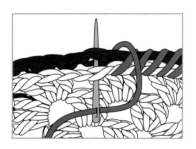

Fig. 10b

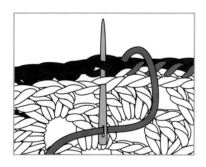

FRINGE

Cut a piece of cardboard 6" (15 cm) wide and ½" (12 mm) longer than you want your finished fringe to be. Wind the yarn **loosely** and **evenly** lengthwise around the cardboard until the card is filled, then cut across one end; repeat as needed.

Hold together as many strands as specified in individual instructions; fold in half.

With **wrong** side facing and using a crochet hook, draw the folded end up through a stitch, space, or row and pull the loose ends through the folded end *(Figs. 11a & c)*; draw the knot up **tightly** *(Figs. 11b & d)*.

Repeat, spacing as specified in individual instructions. Lay Afghan flat on a hard surface and trim the ends.

Fig. 11a

Fig. 11b

Fig. 11c

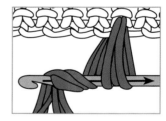

Fig. 11d

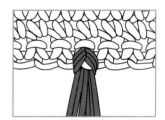

yarn information

Each Afghan in this book was made using Light Weight or Medium Weight Yarn. Any brand of the weight specified may be used. It is best to refer to the yardage/meters when determining how many balls or skeins to purchase. Remember, to arrive at the finished size, it is the GAUGE/TENSION that is important, not the brand of yarn.

For your convenience, listed below are the specific yarns used to create our photography models.

BABY BLUE
Red Heart® Baby Teri™
#9181 Blue

CLUSTER STRIPES
Patons® Canadiana
White - #00001 White
Lavender - #00023 Lilac
Blue - #00029 Lt Blue
Green - #00045 Aqua

BABY LOVES SPRINGTIME
Patons® Astra
Pink - #02752 Baby Pink
Dk Pink - #02210 Deep Pink
White - #02751 White

BIG WHEELS
Red Heart® Classic®
White - #3 Off White
Black - #12 Black
Lt Grey - #401 Nickel
Med Blue - #822 True Blue
Red - #912 Cherry Red
Orange - #245 Orange
Green - #676 Emerald
Blue - #849 Olympic Blue
Red Heart® Kids™
Yellow - #2230 Yellow

BUDS & BLOOMS
Patons® Astra
White - #02751 White
Yellow - #02943 Maize Yellow

CANDY SPRINKLES
Red Heart® TLC® Baby
White - #5011 White
Red Heart® Sport
Orange - #254 Pumpkin
Purple - #585 Purple
Green - #652 Limeade
Pink - #922 Hot Pink

CHERISHED REMINDER
Red Heart® Soft Baby®
#7321 Powder Yellow

HEIRLOOM RUFFLES
Red Heart® Soft Baby®
##7737 Powder Pink

HUGS & HEARTS
Reynolds™ Utopia Sport
White - #2200 White
Green - #2131 Lt Green
Pink - #2295 Lt Pink

LEMON DROP
Bernat® Berella® "4"®
White - #8941 Winter White
Yellow - #8900 Banana

LACY TREASURE
Red Heart® Soft Baby®
#7001 White

LITTLE BOY BLUE
Bernat® Softee® Baby
#30184 Baby Denim

PINEAPPLE PARADE
Bernat® Baby Coordinates
Pink - #01008 Baby Pink
Variegated - #01100 Aqua/Pink

SHINING STAR
Bernat® Satin
#04230 Spring

PINEAPPLE PATCH
Bernat® Baby Coordinates
Variegated - #01200 Fantasy
Yellow - #01011 Lemon Custard

PINK POSIES
Bernat® Softee® Baby
#02001 Pink

SOFT AS SNOW
Bernat® Satin
#04005 Snow

SQUARE FLOWER
Patons® Astra
Yellow - #02943 Maize Yellow
Pink - #02210 Deep Pink

SONNY BOY
Bernat® Baby Coordinates
Blue - #01005 Sky
White - #01000 White

SPRING SPIRALS
Bernat® Satin
White - #04005 Snow
Blue - #04143 Lapis
Pink - #04420 Sea Shell

SQUARE MOTIF WITH FLOWER
Patons® Astra
Blue - #02774 Medium Blue
Red Heart® Sport
Green - #652 Limeade

GRAND PRIZE
Bernat® Cottontots™
White - #90005 Wonder White
Scraps:
#90420 Pretty in Pink
#90230 Sweet Green
#90215 Sweet Aqua
#90510 Sweet Apricot
#90615 Sunshine
#90320 Lovely Lilac

SWEETEST HEARTS
Caron® Simply Soft Baby Sport
White - #2501 White
Pink - #2506 Soft Pink

STORY TIME
Red Heart® TLC® Essentials™
Purple - #2531 Lt Plum
White - #2316 Winter White

TAFFY
Bernat® Berella® "4"®
#8941 Winter White

SWEETHEART ROSES
Bernat® Softee® Baby
Green - #02004 Mint
Pink - #02001 Pink
Bernat® Baby
Pink - #21469 Pink

TENDER HEARTS
Reynolds™ Utopia Sport
#2223 Yellow

STARLIGHT STAR BRIGHT
Bernat® Cottontots™
Variegated - #91713 Koolade
Yellow - #90616 Lemon Berry
Blue - #90129 Blueberry

WAVY STRIPS
Red Heart® Soft Baby®
Lavender - #7588 Lilac
Green - #7624 Lime
White - #7001 White